World Adventure

A Supplement to Childcraft— The How and Why Library

World Book, Inc.
a Scott Fetzer company
Chicago

For information on other World Book products,
visit us at our Web site at http://www.worldbook.com

For information on sales to schools and libraries in the United
States, call 1-800-975-3250.

For information on sales to schools and libraries in Canada,
call 1-800-837-5365.

World Book, Inc.
233 North Michigan Avenue
Chicago, IL 60601
U.S.A.

LC number: 00-101628

ISBN: 7166-0600-3

Printed in the United States of America

1 2 3 4 5 6 7 8 9 06 05 04 03 02 01 00

Staff

Contents

SOUTH AMERICA AND ANTARCTICA

NORTH AMERICA

EUROPE

ASIA

AUSTRALIA AND THE PACIFIC ISLANDS

AFRICA

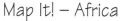

Preface

Where would you like to travel? What parts of your own country would you like to visit, and what other countries would you like to see?

If you are not sure, here is a chance to find out. In **World Adventure,** you will travel around the world with four friends. You will see spots that world travelers often visit and places few travelers ever see. You will find out how to wear a dopy and what *creme de abacate* tastes like—and more.

On your trip around the world, you will be traveling with Gabe, Julia, Steve, and Yoshi. You'll visit seven continents and crisscross most of them by train, plane, car, or boat. You'll cross three big oceans.

At the beginning of each chapter is a map of the friends' travels—with some questions about the interesting things you will find. In each chapter, you will read the journal the four friends kept and see the guidebook information and newspaper clippings they collected, their

Dear Grandma,   January 29
We met a group of schoolchildren today. They taught us games and then gave us each an arpillera. An arpillera is patchwork folk art. Mine looks like the one on the other side of this card!

                    Love,
                    Julia

PERU

GUIDEBOOK/NEW ZEALAND

The first Maori lived by hunting and fishing. They have been named the moa hunters because they mainly hunted moas, giant birds that could not fly. By the 1700's, no moas were left.

Why aren't there any trumpets in a gamelan orchestra?

Does a jeepney fly, roll, or float?

Southeast Asia is located north of Australia, south of China, and east of India. Many Westerners have heard the region's exotic-sounding place names—Bangkok, Bali, and Java, to name a few. But few Westerners know about the land and people of Southeast Asia's countries.

September 12
We arrived in the airport at Laos's capital, Vientiane, in the middle of a downpour. The city lies on the Mekong River. The captain told us that the Mekong flows the entire length of the country. It is the major highway, especially during the rainy season—right now. We didn't have to leave the airport, because we caught a flight north to Louangphrabang.

Welcome to Southeast Asia!

Why do elephants get sent to camp?

Do some frogs really fly?

Southeast Asia

Name the Foal Contest!

The Royal Canadian Mounted Police will have four beautiful new foals, or baby horses, this spring, and children will get to help name them. Each child should suggest one name. It should start with the letter R, as in Royal, and be no longer than six letters. Enter your idea today!

shoppers at an outdoor market in Cusco, Peru

Creme de abacate from Brazil

In a blender, mix:
1 large peeled and pitted avocado,
2 tablespoons of fresh lime juice, and
2 to 3 tablespoons of granulated sugar.
Serve in a fancy glass. Decorate with a sprig of mint.

snapshots, and the postcards they sent. By the time you have traveled partway through the book, you'll be a very savvy traveler.

Maps are included in this book to help you see where your travels with Gabe, Julia, Steve, and Yoshi are taking you.

The map at the beginning of each chapter shows all the places the four friends plan to go in one region. Just follow the broken red line. If you ever get lost along the way, use the regional map to locate the place you are looking for.

You will find more maps throughout the chapter that show cities and other places and things. You can use those maps to locate interesting spots that you read

Angel Falls in Venezuela

PHRASE BOOK

Mediterranean is a Latin word meaning "in the middle of land."

about. On the next few pages, you will find a **World Map Index** and a detailed **Map of the World.**

For a break from your travels, try the activities in each chapter and the **Map It!** puzzle at the end of each continent. At the back of the book, you'll find important or unusual words defined in the **Glossary.** Other resources about interesting places to visit are listed in the section called **Find Out More.** Use the **Index** to look up places and things that interest you the most.

Have fun on your trip. You will discover some things that most people don't know and find ideas for planning a trip of your own. Are you ready?

World Map Index

SOUTH AMERICA

Country	Capital	Map Key
Argentina	Buenos Aires	G 6
Bolivia	La Paz; Sucre	F 6
Brazil	Brasília	F 7
Chile	Santiago	G 6
Colombia	Bogotá	E 6
Ecuador	Quito	F 6
Guyana	Georgetown	E 7
Paraguay	Asunción	G 7
Peru	Lima	F 6
Suriname	Paramaribo	E 7
Uruguay	Montevideo	G 7
Venezuela	Caracas	E 6

ANTARCTICA

There are no countries in Antarctica.

NORTH AMERICA

Country	Capital	Map Key
Antigua and Barbuda	St. John's	E6
Bahamas	Nassau	D6
Barbados	Bridgetown	E7
Belize	Belmopan	E5
Canada	Ottawa	C4
Costa Rica	San José	E5
Cuba	Havana	D5
Dominica	Roseau	E6
Dominican Republic	Santo Domingo	E6
El Salvador	San Salvador	E5
Grenada	St. George's	E6
Guatemala	Guatemala City	E5
Haiti	Port-au-Prince	E6
Honduras	Tegucigalpa	E5
Jamaica	Kingston	E6
Mexico	Mexico City	D4
Nicaragua	Managua	E5
Panama	Panama City	E5
St. Kitts and Nevis	Basseterre	E6‡
St. Lucia	Castries	E6
St. Vincent and the Grenadines	Kingstown	E6
Trinidad and Tobago	Port-of-Spain	E6
United States	Washington, D.C.	C4

EUROPE

Country	Capital	Map Key
Albania	Tiranë	C11
Andorra	Andorra la Vella	C10‡
Austria	Vienna	C10
Belarus	Minsk	C12
Belgium	Brussels	C10
Bosnia-Herzegovina	Sarajevo	C10
Bulgaria	Sofia	C11
Croatia	Zagreb	C10
Czech Republic	Prague	C10
Denmark	Copenhagen	C10
Estonia	Tallinn	C11
Finland	Helsinki	B11
France	Paris	C10
Germany	Berlin	C10
Greece	Athens	D11
Hungary	Budapest	C10
Iceland	Reykjavík	B9
Ireland	Dublin	C9
Italy	Rome	C10
Latvia	Riga	C11
Liechtenstein	Vaduz	C10
Lithuania	Vilnius	C11
Luxembourg	Luxembourg	C10
Macedonia	Skopje	C10
Malta	Valletta	D10
Moldova	Chisinau	C11
Monaco	Monaco	C10‡
Netherlands	Amsterdam	C10
Norway	Oslo	B10
Poland	Warsaw	C10
Portugal	Lisbon	D9
Romania	Bucharest	C11
Russia (European)	Moscow	C13
San Marino	San Marino	C10‡
Slovakia	Bratislava	C11
Slovenia	Ljubljana	C11
Spain	Madrid	C9
Sweden	Stockholm	B10
Switzerland	Bern	C10
Ukraine	Kiev	C11
United Kingdom	London	C9
Vatican City	—	C10‡
Yugoslavia	Belgrade	C10

Use the map key to find a country on the world map shown on pages 14 and 15. Countries with this symbol ‡ are too small to be shown on the map. The key shows the area in which they are located.

ASIA

Country	Capital	Map Key
Afghanistan	Kabul	D11
Armenia	Yerevan	D13
Azerbaijan	Baku	D13
Bahrain	Manama	D12
Bangladesh	Dhaka	D14
Bhutan	Thimphu	D14
Brunei	Bandar Seri Begawan	E15
Cambodia	Phnom Penh	E15
China	Beijing	D14
Cyprus	Nicosia	D11
Georgia	Tbilisi	D12
India	New Delhi	D13
Indonesia	Jakarta	F16
Iran	Teheran	D12
Iraq	Baghdad	D12
Israel	Jerusalem	D11
Japan	Tokyo	D16
Jordan	Amman	D11
Kazakhstan	Astana	C13
Korea, North	Pyongyang	C16
Korea, South	Seoul	D16
Kuwait	Kuwait	D12
Kyrgyzstan	Bishkek	C15
Laos	Vientiane	E15
Lebanon	Beirut	D11
Malaysia	Kuala Lumpur	E15
Maldives	Male	E13
Mongolia	Ulan Bator	C15
Myanmar	Yangon	D14
Nepal	Kathmandu	D14
Oman	Muscat	E12
Pakistan	Islamabad	D13
Philippines	Manila	E16
Qatar	Doha	D12
Russia (Asian)	Moscow	C13
Saudi Arabia	Riyadh	D12
Singapore	Singapore	E15
Sri Lanka	Colombo	E14
Syria	Damascus	D11
Taiwan	Taipei	D16
Tajikistan	Dushanbe	D14
Thailand	Bangkok	E15
Turkey	Ankara	D11
Turkmenistan	Ashgabat	D13
United Arab Emirates	Abu Dhabi	D12
Uzbekistan	Tashkent	D14
Vietnam	Hanoi	E15
Yemen	Sana	E12

AUSTRALIA AND THE PACIFIC ISLANDS

Country	Capital	Map Key
Australia	Canberra	G16
Fiji	Suva	F1
Kiribati	Tarawa	F1
Marshall Islands	Majuro	E18
Micronesia, Federated States of	Palikir	E17
Nauru	—	F18
New Zealand	Wellington	G18
Palau	Koror	E16
Papua New Guinea	Port Moresby	F17
Samoa	Apia	F1
Solomon Islands	Honiara	F18
Tonga	Nukualofa	F1
Tuvalu	Funafuti	F1
Vanuatu	Port-Vila	F18

AFRICA

Country	Capital	Map Key
Algeria	Algiers	D10
Angola	Luanda	F10
Benin	Porto-Novo	E10
Botswana	Gaborone	G11
Burkina Faso	Ouagadougou	E9
Burundi	Bujumbura	F11
Cameroon	Yaoundé	E10
Cape Verde	Praia	E8
Central African Republic	Bangui	E10
Chad	N'Djamena	E10
Comoros	Moroni	F12
Congo (Brazzaville)	Brazzaville	F10
Congo (Kinshasa)	Kinshasa	F11
Côte d'Ivoire (Ivory Coast)	Yamoussoukro, Abidjan	E9
Djibouti	Djibouti	E12
Egypt	Cairo	D11
Equatorial Guinea	Malabo	E10
Eritrea	Asmara	E12
Estonia	Tallinn	C11
Ethiopia	Addis Ababa	E11
Gabon	Libreville	F10
Gambia	Banjul	E9
Ghana	Accra	E9
Guinea	Conakry	E9
Guinea-Bissau	Bissau	E9
Kenya	Nairobi	E11
Lesotho	Maseru	G11
Liberia	Monrovia	E9
Libya	Tripoli	D10
Madagascar	Antananarivo	F12
Malawi	Lilongwe	F11
Mali	Bamako	E9
Mauritania	Nouakchott	D9
Mauritius	Port Louis	G12
Morocco	Rabat	D9
Mozambique	Maputo	F11
Namibia	Windhoek	G11
Niger	Niamey	E10
Nigeria	Abuja	E10
Rwanda	Kigali	F11
São Tomé and Príncipe	São Tomé	E10
Senegal	Dakar	E9
Seychelles	Victoria	F12
Sierra Leone	Freetown	E9
Somalia	Mogadishu	E12
South Africa	Cape Town; Pretoria; Bloemfontein	G11
Sudan	Khartoum	E11
Swaziland	Mbabane	G11
Tanzania	Dar es Salaam	F11
Togo	Lomé	E9
Tunisia	Tunis	D10
Uganda	Kampala	E11
Zambia	Lusaka	F11
Zimbabwe	Harare	G11

Map of the World

A table that lists countries, capitals, and a key to this map is on pages 11, 12, and 13.

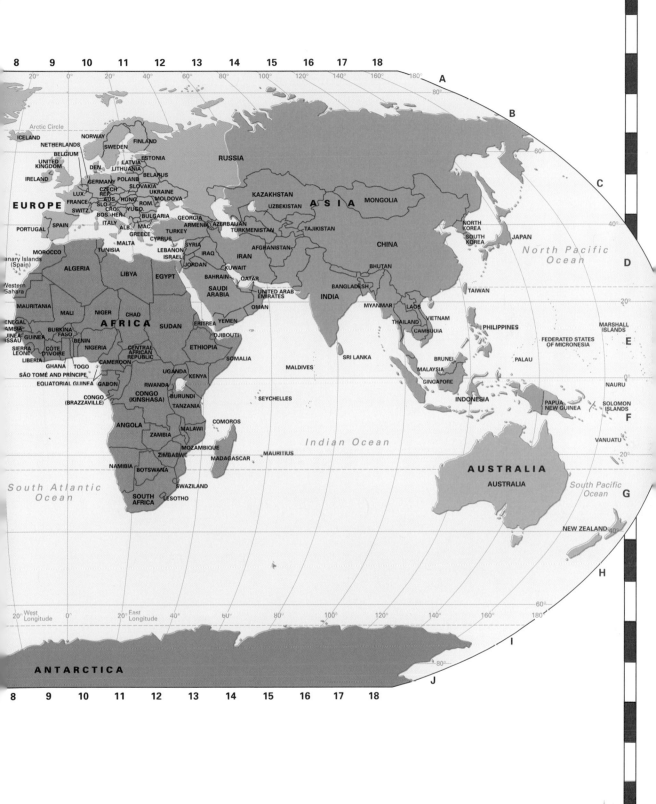

20° 0° 20° 40° 60° 80° 100° 120° 140° 160° 180°

A

80°

B

Arctic Circle

60°

ICELAND
NORWAY
NETHERLANDS
BELGIUM
SWEDEN
FINLAND
ESTONIA
UNITED
KINGDOM
DEN.
LATVIA
LITHUANIA
RUSSIA

C

IRELAND
GERMANY
POLAND
BELARUS

CZECH
REP.
SLOVAKIA
UKRAINE
KAZAKHSTAN
MONGOLIA

40°

EUROPE
FRANCE
LUX.
SLO.
AUS.
HUNG.
MOLDOVA
ROM.
UZBEKISTAN
A S I A

SWITZ.
CRO.
YUGO.
BULGARIA

PORTUGAL
SPAIN
ITALY
ALB.
MAC.
GEORGIA
ARMENIA
AZERBAIJAN
TAJIKISTAN

NORTH
KOREA
JAPAN

GREECE
CYPRUS
TURKEY
TURKMENISTAN
SOUTH
KOREA

D

Western
Sahara
MOROCCO
MALTA
TUNISIA
LEBANON
ISRAEL
SYRIA
IRAQ
AFGHANISTAN
CHINA

North Pacific
Ocean

20°

ALGERIA
LIBYA
EGYPT
JORDAN
KUWAIT
IRAN
BHUTAN

anary Islands
(Spain)

MAURITANIA
BAHRAIN
QATAR
BANGLADESH
TAIWAN

MALI
NIGER
CHAD
SAUDI
ARABIA
UNITED ARAB
EMIRATES
INDIA
MYANMAR
LAOS

0°

ENEGAL
MBIA
BURKINA
FASO
A F R I C A
SUDAN
OMAN
THAILAND
VIETNAM

JINEA
ISSAU
GUINEA
BENIN
ERITREA
YEMEN
CAMBODIA

PHILIPPINES

MARSHALL
ISLANDS

E

SIERRA
LEONE
CÔTE
D'IVOIRE
NIGERIA
DJIBOUTI

LIBERIA
CENTRAL
AFRICAN
REPUBLIC
ETHIOPIA

FEDERATED STATES
OF MICRONESIA

GHANA
TOGO
CAMEROON
SOMALIA
MALDIVES
SRI LANKA

BRUNEI
PALAU

NAURU

SÃO TOMÉ AND PRÍNCIPE
UGANDA
KENYA
MALAYSIA

EQUATORIAL GUINEA
GABON
RWANDA
SINGAPORE

CONGO
(BRAZZAVILLE)
CONGO
(KINSHASA)
BURUNDI
TANZANIA
SEYCHELLES
INDONESIA
PAPUA
NEW GUINEA

SOLOMON
ISLANDS

F

ANGOLA
MALAWI
COMOROS

ZAMBIA
MOZAMBIQUE
VANUATU

Indian Ocean

ZIMBABWE
MADAGASCAR
MAURITIUS

20°

South Atlantic
Ocean
NAMIBIA
BOTSWANA
AUSTRALIA

AUSTRALIA
South Pacific
Ocean

G

SWAZILAND

SOUTH
AFRICA
LESOTHO

NEW ZEALAND
40°

H

60°

20° West
Longitude
0°
20° East
Longitude
40°
60°
80°
100°
120°
140°
160°
180°

I

80°

ANTARCTICA

J

Paraguay, Uruguay, Chile, and Argentina make up the "southern cone" of South America. In much of this region, the climate resembles the climate of Europe—an upside down Europe, that is. When Europe is having winter, the "cone" is enjoying summer. Whatever the season, the southern tip of South America is as cold as northernmost Europe. In fact, south of the "cone" lies the coldest place on Earth—the continent of Antarctica.

Easter Island

January 2

Today we landed on the rugged, windy island at the tip of the "southern cone." We're staying in Ushuaia. This town and nearby Puerto Williams are the southernmost towns on Earth.

Welcome to Southern South America and Antarctica!

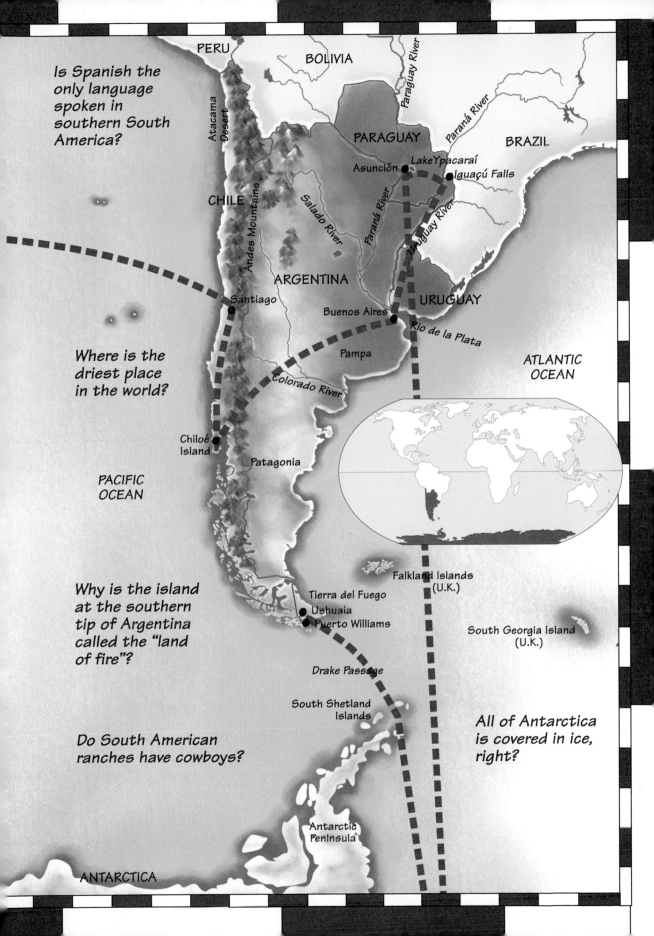

Is Spanish the only language spoken in southern South America?

Where is the driest place in the world?

Why is the island at the southern tip of Argentina called the "land of fire"?

Do South American ranches have cowboys?

All of Antarctica is covered in ice, right?

PERU

BOLIVIA

Paraguay River

Paraná River

BRAZIL

PARAGUAY

Asunción

LakeYpacaraí

Iguaçú Falls

CHILE

Atacama Desert

Andes Mountains

Salado River

Paraná River

Uruguay River

ARGENTINA

URUGUAY

Santiago

Buenos Aires

Rio de la Plata

ATLANTIC OCEAN

Pampa

Colorado River

Chiloé Island

Patagonia

PACIFIC OCEAN

Falkland Islands (U.K.)

Tierra del Fuego

Ushuaia

Puerto Williams

South Georgia Island (U.K.)

Drake Passage

South Shetland Islands

Antarctic Peninsula

ANTARCTICA

January 3

We sailed across the Drake Passage toward Antarctica. We were looking for humpbacks, minkes, and other whales that spend summers in Antarctic waters. Steven had read that whales breathe through blowholes in their heads, and their warm breath forms misty columns as it hits the cold air. We could not see any whales, but Steven pointed out several tall spouts in the distance. That was really exciting!

January 5

At the South Shetland Islands, we boarded a smaller boat so we could steer around floating ice on our way to the Antarctic Peninsula. On the ice, thousands of emperor penguins fussed over their white-faced chicks. One chick hopped in the water, and a Weddell seal popped out and nearly gobbled it up. The seal may have been waiting underwater for almost an hour. That's how long it can hold its breath!

January 9

We've been visiting researchers in the McMurdo dry valleys. The researchers told us that most of Antarctica's land lies under ice up to 3 miles thick. But strong winds have blasted away the snow in the dry valleys and have stopped ice from forming on the ground.

Early natives on the islands kept fires blazing to stay warm. In 1520 Portuguese explorer Ferdinand Magellan spied the fires as his ship neared the tip of South America. He named the islands Tierra del Fuego, which means "land of fire."

Researchers here are collecting 180-million-year-old rock samples. They're even collecting algae from lakes! Because the average temperature is well below freezing, most Antarctic lakes are frozen to the bottom. But in the dry valleys, algae grow in warm water trapped beneath only a few feet of ice.

Iceberg Floats North

An enormous iceberg is drifting north from Antarctica. Ships may have to detour more than 100 miles (161 kilometers) to stay clear.

Dear Grandma,
Beautiful hankies of ñanduti,
or spiderweb lace, cost just
pennies. In the town of
Itauguá, Paraguay, all
women, even little girls,
make lace.

Julia

Paraguay

January 11

We almost wish we were back in Antarctica! Summer in Asunción, Paraguay, is steamy. A local shopkeeper suggested a trip to Lake Ypacaraí to cool off. Before leaving, we bought corn cakes called *chipas* from a Guaraní woman. The Guaraní are Paraguay's native people, and most Paraguayans have at least one Guaraní ancestor. Paraguay has two official languages, Guaraní and Spanish.

We ate aboard a train pulled by a steam locomotive. It took us through the swampy edge of town and out to the high, cool lakeshore. A jungle of flowering plants surrounds the lake. Lots of people from Asunción were out water-skiing.

gauchos herding cattle on a ranch in Uruguay

January 12

We headed to the Argentine border to watch tons of water roar over Iguaçú Falls. Actually, Iguaçú is made up of 300 waterfalls! A permanent rainbow hangs in the cloud of spray overhead. Yoshi took lots of pictures. We hope they show the rainbow.

January 13

Yesterday we arrived at an *estancia,* a cattle ranch, in Uruguay. The owners treated us to milk, honey, and *chivitos.* Chivitos are steak sandwiches with cheese, lettuce, tomato, and bacon. Everything, even the honey, was produced here on the ranch.

After dinner, we met some gauchos— cowboys! They offered us wide-brimmed hats and helped us saddle several chestnut-colored *criollos.* These horses are like North American mustangs. Their ancestors arrived with the Spanish, escaped to the wild, and developed into a new, tough breed. We didn't herd cattle, but we enjoyed seeing the gauchos swing their *boleadores.*

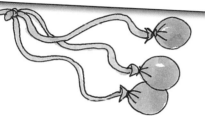

PHRASE BOOK

Boleadores (boh lay ah DOHR ehs) are three balls connected by ropes. Gauchos throw them at the animal they are chasing, and the ropes wrap around the animal's hind legs.

January 14

We took a ferry across the Rio de la Plata to Buenos Aires. The houses near the dock were painted the colors of fruit. We heard tango music everywhere—at

Easter Island

cafes, on radios, and in the streets. A cafe owner told us that in the 1800's, Argentine gauchos, African Americans, and European immigrants from poor parts of the city created the steps to the dance called the tango. He said that tango music has become the most popular music in Argentina.

January 15

Today we took a bus across the Pampa. The Pampa is a treeless plain in the middle of Argentina. Fields of grain were all we saw for miles and miles. The bus climbed onto a plateau (pla TOH), a high flat area, called Patagonia. The wind blew so strongly that the trees looked as if they were looking sideways. Near one tree

colorfully decorated houses in the port area of Buenos Aires, Argentina

grazed a guanaco, the camel's South American cousin. It looks like a small, cinnamon-colored camel with no hump.

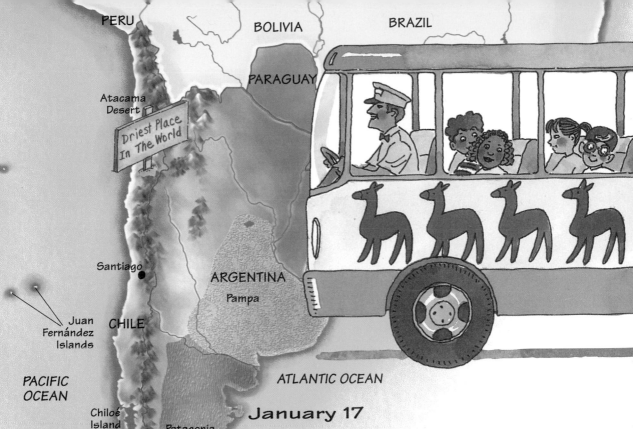

PERU
BOLIVIA
BRAZIL
PARAGUAY
Atacama Desert
Driest Place In The World
Santiago
ARGENTINA
Pampa
Juan Fernández Islands
CHILE
PACIFIC OCEAN
ATLANTIC OCEAN
Chiloé Island
Patagonia

January 17

We crossed into Chile and stopped at the island of Chiloé. The people there told us of a magic ship that lures fishermen far out to sea. From Chiloé we flew to Santiago. We took a bus to Isla Negra and visited the home of Pablo Neruda, Chile's most famous Nobel Prize-winning poet.

January 19

From Santiago we flew to Easter Island, a possession of Chile far out in the Pacific. The island has a population of about 2,000 people and hundreds of *moai*. These are giant heads that islanders cut from volcanic rock about 1,500 years ago. On the return flight, we passed over the island where Alexander Selkirk was marooned for four years. His story inspired Daniel Defoe's *Robinson Crusoe*.

ROBINSON CRUSOE

Southern South America and Antarctica 23

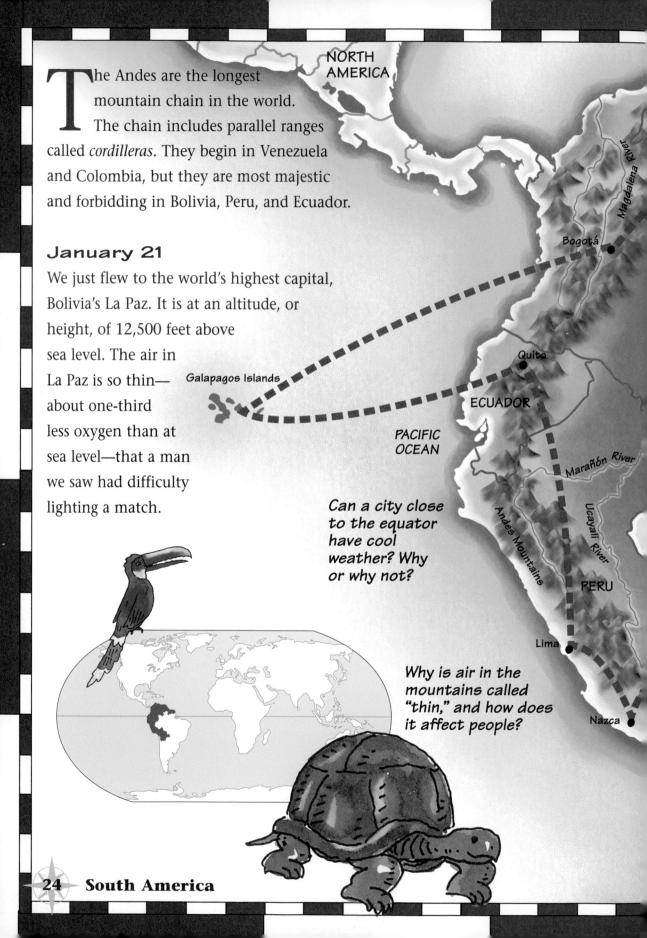

The Andes are the longest mountain chain in the world. The chain includes parallel ranges called *cordilleras*. They begin in Venezuela and Colombia, but they are most majestic and forbidding in Bolivia, Peru, and Ecuador.

January 21

We just flew to the world's highest capital, Bolivia's La Paz. It is at an altitude, or height, of 12,500 feet above sea level. The air in La Paz is so thin—about one-third less oxygen than at sea level—that a man we saw had difficulty lighting a match.

Can a city close to the equator have cool weather? Why or why not?

Why is air in the mountains called "thin," and how does it affect people?

NORTH AMERICA

Magdalena River

Bogotá

Quito

Galapagos Islands

ECUADOR

PACIFIC OCEAN

Marañón River

Ucayali River

Andes Mountains

PERU

Lima

Nazca

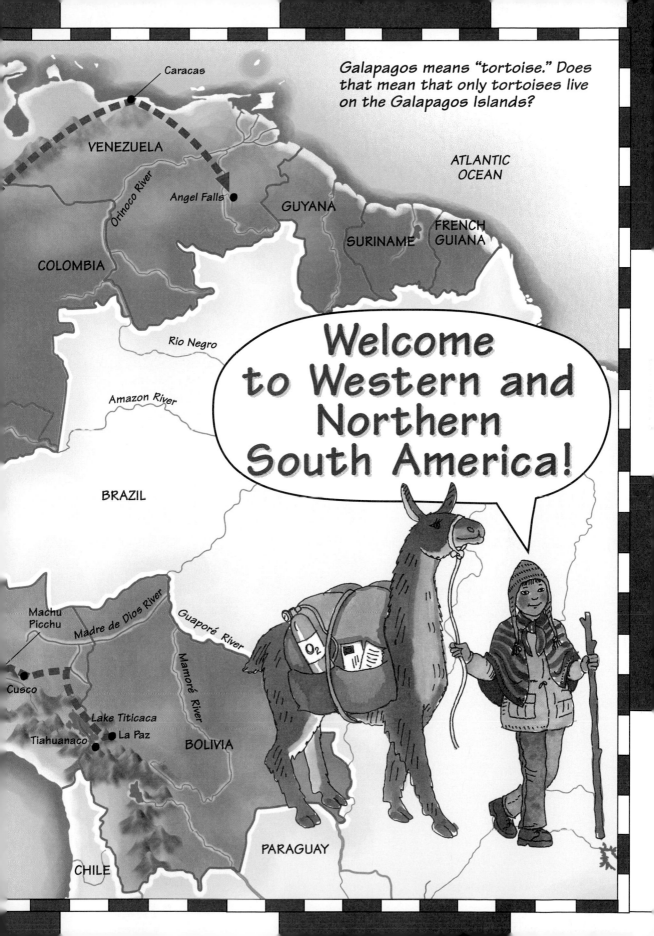

January 22

We rode a bus west from La Paz to Tiahuanaco. These ruins were once the home of the Tiwanaku people, who fished, herded llamas (another relative of the camel), and grew potatoes. As many as 40,000 people lived there. Nearly 2,000 years ago, they began to build large stone structures that still stand. The most impressive is the Gateway of

The Gateway of the Sun at Tiahuanaco, Bolivia, probably was a monument to a god or ruler of the Tiwanaku.

the Sun. Farmers probably built the structures as a monument to their god or ruler. About 800 years ago, the Tiwanaku vanished. No one knows why.

January 23

The bus took us north to Lake Titicaca, the world's highest navigable lake. Many people there travel in boats made from bundles of reeds that grow in the lake. People who lived in the area were building reed boats long before explorers arrived in South America.

About 450 years after the Spaniards arrived in the area, a Norwegian explorer named Thor Heyerdahl approached boat builders on the island of Suriki in Lake Titicaca. He asked them to build *Ra II*. In 1970, Heyerdahl and a crew sailed the boat across the Atlantic to show that ancient Egyptians could have used such boats to travel to the Americas. Heyerdahl's boat is on display in Norway, but its builders run a museum on Suriki. A fisherman ferried us to the island. We looked at the plans for the *Ra II,* and Gabe bought a model of the reed boat that brought us.

Dizzy? Like many tourists, you may be suffering from *sóroche*, or altitude sickness, and thin air. What's the cure? A cup of *maté de coca*, tea brewed from herbs and coca leaf.

January 24

We crossed to the Peruvian side of Lake Titicaca and hopped the train for Cusco. Julia picked up a leaflet at a tourist booth. It says that this city is at least 600 years old. First, it was the capital of the Inca, who ruled an empire that stretched from eastern Colombia to central Chile. Then the Spanish seized it in 1533. Today most of the 140,000 people in Cusco are *mestizos,* who have both Europeans and Native Americans for ancestors. In fact, Spanish and *Quechua,* the language of the Inca, are both official languages of Peru.

shoppers at an outdoor market in Cusco, Peru

January 25

Julia insisted that we hike the Inca Trail to the ruins of Machu Picchu. That's an Inca archaeological site. But our guide warned us that January is rainy season, and the trail would be much too dangerous to hike. So we took the bus instead.

At first, all we saw were scrubby bushes and a few straw huts. The huts probably were like the houses of people who first settled in the highlands to raise llamas, beans, and peppers 7,000 years ago. Then we came upon some of the Inca stone ruins. A guide pointed out that the Chavín and Moche cultures in northern Peru built temples of rock and stone hundreds of years before the Inca. The Moche were also master metal workers and crafted fine gold jewelry.

The bus stopped and we got out. We climbed a stone stairway built by the early Incas. The surrounding country is a thick forest. Finally we reached Machu Picchu. The guide said that it was probably used as a home for members of the Inca royal family when they were away from Cusco.

PHRASE BOOK

Machu Picchu means "Old Peak," and the mountain that looms over it is Huayna Picchu, or "Young Peak."

The buildings used to have thatch roofs to protect the people inside from the frequent rains. But the place is hardly "ruins" because the buildings are still standing. The Inca may not have been the first stone masons in the Andes, but they probably were the best. The building blocks interlock like puzzle pieces and have stayed together for about 600 years without mortar.

January 28

We boarded a plane to Lima, Peru's capital. Due to bad weather in the mountains, the pilot had to fly southward. That was lucky for us, because we got to see the strange patterns of lines on the ground near the town of Nazca, Peru. These patterns in the sand are almost 2,000 years old and can be viewed only from the air. Gabe spotted them right away. He pointed out the outlines of a bird, a monkey, and a fish.

Math Solves Mystery

Author Maria Reiche, a German mathematician, spent more than 50 years measuring and analyzing the Nazca lines. In her book *Mystery on the Desert,* Reiche explains her theory about the lines. She believes ancient Peruvians drew them as a calendar for their gods to follow in sending good weather for their crops.

Dear Grandma,   January 29
We met a group of schoolchildren today. They taught us games and then gave us each an arpillera. An arpillera is patchwork folk art. Mine looks like the one on the other side of this card!

Love,
Julia

PERU

January 30

We spent the night at the clay and thatch lodge that the Ese'eja natives have built near the Tambopata-Candamo wildlife reserve. In the morning, we explored the rain forest, looking for some of the area's 1,200 species, or kinds, of butterflies; 90 species of frogs; and 32 species of parrots. After a long boat trip, we reached a clay lick. It is a ledge of very salty clay where macaws, a kind of parrot, get the salt they need in their diets. Everywhere we looked, the riverbank was covered with the bright rainbow colors of these birds.

January 31

Quito, Ecuador, is cool! We know that lands near the equator are the warmest on earth, But Quito's temperature is mild, never hot. Our guidebook says that's because the city is nearly 2 miles above sea level. Temperatures drop 4 degrees for every 1,000 feet that the land is above sea level.

Pinta

Marchena

Genovesa

GALAPAGOS ISLANDS

equator

San Salvador

Fernandina

Pinzón

Santa Cruz

Santa Fe

Isabela

Charles Darwin Research Center

Santa María

February 3

The more than 20 islands in the Galapagos once served as prison colonies and pirate hideaways. The government of Ecuador has since made them a national park, open to visitors but not to settlers.

A naturalist, or expert on wildlife, guided us around the Galapagos. First stop on the tour was Santa María Island. Tortoises, which gave the islands their name, nest on its beaches. Flocks of flamingos feed in its lagoons. Penguins live on Isabela, the largest island. Marine iguanas and flightless cormorants, a kind of sea bird, inhabit Fernandina. My favorite bird here is the blue-footed booby, who attracts his mate by showing her his feet.

The last stop was Española, where green turtles come ashore only at night. They leave their eggs to hatch in the sun's warmth. Unfortunately, the wild dogs, pigs, goats, and cats that roam the island eat turtle eggs. One job of naturalists from the Charles Darwin Research Center on Santa Cruz Island is to protect the eggs.

GUIDEBOOK/ECUADOR

Naturalist Charles Darwin came to the Galapagos in 1835. The islands' wildlife fascinated him. He counted 13 kinds of finches, each with a different beak specially shaped for gathering the food it needed. Observations like this helped Darwin form his theory of evolution, which explains the development of animals over the ages. Above are some of the finches Darwin studied and some of the notes he wrote about wildlife in the Galapagos.

San Cristóbal

Española

GUIDEBOOK/COLOMBIA

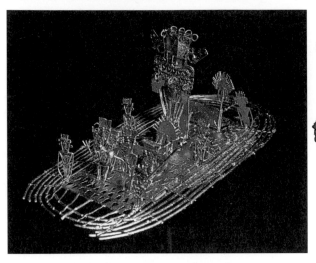

The legend of El Dorado was based on a people who lived in what is now Colombia. During coronation ceremonies, they covered their new king in gold dust and threw offerings of gold statues into Lake Guatavita.

February 4

This morning our plane landed in Bogotá, the capital of Colombia. On the ride from El Dorado airport, we passed miles of greenhouses where Colombians grow flowers that they export, or send to other countries to sell.

The Museo del Oro in Bogotá has great exhibits of another

Colombian export—gold! Early native craftspeople made the thousands of gold statues, masks, rings, bracelets, and earrings on display at the museum. Early Spanish settlers heard legends about El Dorado from Incas and other groups. They thought it was a kingdom of gold. But Spaniards never thought to look for

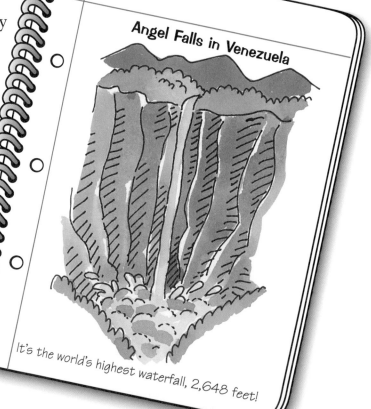

Angel Falls in Venezuela

It's the world's highest waterfall, 2,648 feet!

gold by digging up the sites of old towns. So archaeologists uncovered treasures in Colombia centuries after Spanish conquerors had come and gone.

Many poor people live in small huts, or ranchos, in the hills around Caracas, Venezuela.

February 6

This morning we arrived in Caracas, the capital of Venezuela. From the airport, we saw hundreds of tiny, roughly built huts clinging to the hillsides around the city. Later we found out that these are the *ranchos* of migrants from the countryside. They came to Caracas looking for jobs and found none. Now the government is trying to build up industry and agriculture to make more jobs.

Some people have good jobs and money to spend at the shopping malls and restaurants in town. At one restaurant, Steven ordered squid served in its own ink. The rest of us ate hamburgers.

Brazil has almost one-half the land in South America. This vast country includes white beaches, wild marshlands, old cities like Rio de Janeiro, futuristic cities like the capital Brasília, and rain forests on its coasts and at its heart. Brazilians have European, African, and Native American backgrounds.

February 10

We arrived by plane at the mouth of the Amazon River in Macapá, Brazil. Then we took a boat north until we met a smaller river, the Araguari. This river rushes into the Atlantic Ocean with great force. At certain times when the Atlantic tide roars in, the two waters make a *pororoca*, a combination of crashing waters and 15-foot waves as high as a two-story house.

Would a piranha rather eat you or a fish?

GUYANA

VENEZUELA

COLOMBIA

Rio Negro

Amazon River (Solimões)

Manaus

PERU

What is Brazil's official language?

BOLIVIA

Madeira River

Why do so many people talk about saving the rain forest?

PARAGUAY

What happens at Carnival in Rio de Janeiro?

What is a snake farm, and why would people raise snakes?

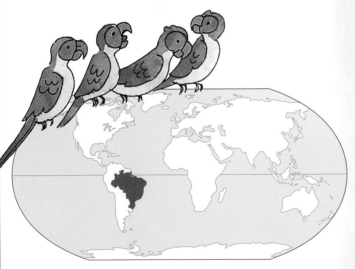

Welcome to Brazil!
SURINAME
FRENCH GUIANA
Macapá
Amazon River
Belém
Marajó Island
Xingu River
Tocantins River
São Francisco
BRAZIL
Salvador
Brasília
Paraná River
São Paulo
Rio de Janeiro
ATLANTIC OCEAN
URUGUAY

February 12

Yesterday we joined a cruise up the Amazon River. As the boat glided through the water, it pushed aside lily pads about as big as a bed! For a close-up look at the river's animal life, our guide netted stingrays and piranhas, a kind of meat-eating fish. He told us that piranhas prefer small fish, frogs, and salamanders to humans. Then he returned the fish to the water. On either side of the river, toucans and flocks of parakeets screeched in the treetops.

The guide pointed out that the Amazon rain forest contains more plant and animal species than any other place on earth. But in the last 30 years, more than one-tenth of the rain forest has been cleared for timber, cattle, crops, and roads. When trees were cut, whole species vanished. Even the water is endangered. Workers flush harmful substances into the streams and poison the river life.

Native Americans in the rain forest are also threatened. Some of these South American Indians have lived there for thousands of years. But ranchers and poor farmers say that they need land to live, too. Our guide suggested ways to use the forest's resources without destroying the forest. For example, Native Americans and other Brazilians might earn their living by harvesting the forest's rubber, Brazil nuts, and medicinal plants rather than its trees.

At night we slept in hammocks on the boat's upper deck. The sound of the engine and the chirping of insects lulled us to sleep.

February 15

While cruising down a part of the Amazon River, we saw black water on the north side of the boat and brown water on the south side. That's because the two main

Manaus Teatro Amazonas, the opera house in Manaus, Brazil

branches of the Amazon, the black Rio Negro and the brown Rio Solimoes, flow side by side—without mixing! The next surprise was at the busy port of Manaus. The port's lavish opera house seemed odd in a city where many houses are just shacks on stilts. According to our guide, "rubber barons" built the opera house in the late 1800's. The air-filled rubber tire had just been invented, and the rubber barons made fortunes supplying tire makers with rubber from the rain forest.

February 17

Here we are in Rio de Janeiro at its most exciting time—
Carnival. Carnival comes right before the six weeks called
Lent, during which Christians fast and pray. Carnival
ends on Fat Tuesday, the day before Lent begins. Roman
Catholics from Portugal brought Carnival to Brazil in the
1500's. At first, people threw flour, mud, and water at
passers-by. Today Carnival is much, much more.

All over the city,
Cariocas—people of
Rio—are preparing for
the big samba contest.
Samba is the favorite
dance music of Brazil.
Africans who arrived
in Brazil as slaves
brought the rhythms
that samba grew out
of. At Carnival, the
beat of the samba
drums puts dancers
into a shaking
frenzy.

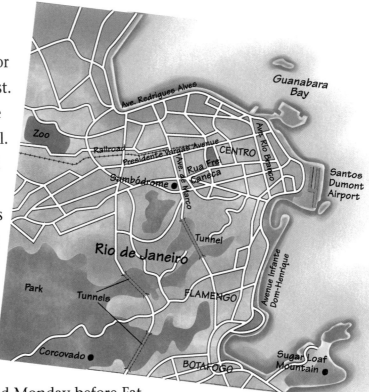

On the Sunday and Monday before Fat
Tuesday, samba schools parade to the Sambódrome, an
auditorium built especially for Carnival. Most people
watch the samba contests. But we decided to join the
parade.

Afterward, we had a green dessert called creme de
abacate. We're bringing home the recipe.

**Creme de abacate
from Brazil**

In a blender, mix:
1 large peeled and pitted avocado,
2 tablespoons of fresh lime juice, and
2 to 3 tablespoons of granulated sugar.
Serve in a fancy glass. Decorate with a
sprig of mint.

February 18

Samba schools welcome tourists who buy and wear the costumes that their members wear. We had a hard time agreeing on a costume.

Yoshi's favorite was the bat. The black feathers on the headdress make the wearer look 8 feet tall. She thought it would be neat for us to flap our wings to the samba beat. But those costumes were so expensive! Finally we settled on the fish, shrimp, and crab costumes. They cost less, and our headdresses had seafood-shaped decorations—and bigger feathers than the bat costumes.

February 19

After Carnival, the buzz around our hotel was about *futebol*, or Brazilian soccer. So we hopped a bus to Maracanã, Rio's huge sports stadium. The teams were good, but the real show was in the stands. The fans cheered their teams by shouting, chanting, and pounding samba drums. One spectator set off fireworks in her team's colors.

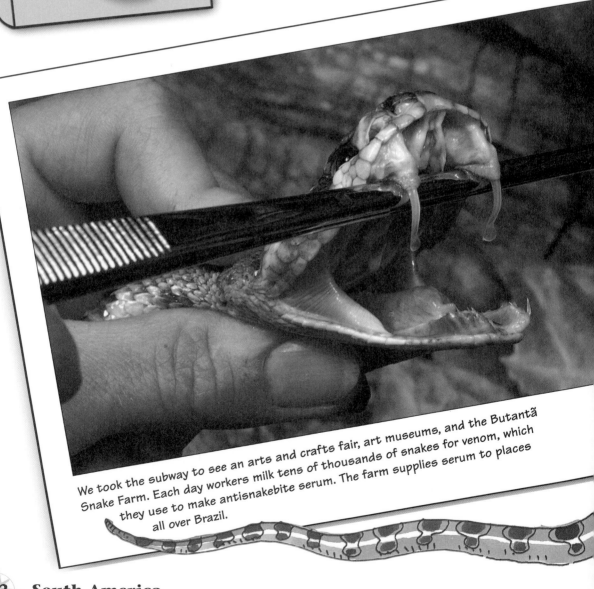

We took the subway to see an arts and crafts fair, art museums, and the Butantã Snake Farm. Each day workers milk tens of thousands of snakes for venom, which they use to make antisnakebite serum. The farm supplies serum to places all over Brazil.

February 21

Yesterday morning we arrived in São Paolo. The city and its suburbs are huge and sprawling. *Paulistanos*—the city's people—have come from all over. Italians arrived in the late 1800's, and Japanese early in the 1900's. Today the São Paolo area is home to about 17 million people. Many work in factories. Seven out of 10 Brazilian-made automobiles are made in São Paolo. When we heard that, we expected major traffic jams. But luckily São Paolo has a clean, fast subway system.

February 22

From São Paolo, we flew northeast to Salvador. On almost every corner, we saw a Catholic church built in the 1500's or 1600's. While visiting one, we noticed carvings of strange figures among the saints. A guide told us that the Portuguese forced African slaves to make the decorations in the churches. The workers inserted images of their African gods.

Descendants of these Africans have formed their own worship groups, or cults, and carry on religious rituals brought from Africa. In Salvador these rituals are called Candomblé. We attended a service last night at a Candomblé center. The leaders wore bright clothes. Some people played drums, and others trembled in a prayerful trance.

MAP IT! South America and Antarctica

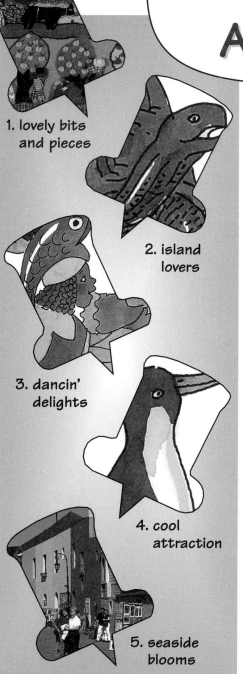

1. lovely bits and pieces

2. island lovers

3. dancin' delights

4. cool attraction

5. seaside blooms

We did it. We traveled all the way across our first two continents— South America and Antarctica. See the giant thumbtacks on this page? Inside each one is a picture clue of one of our favorite places in South America and Antarctica. If the thumbtacks were real, could you pin each one correctly on the map to show where the pictured place is? We drew the route to remind you of where our travels took us.

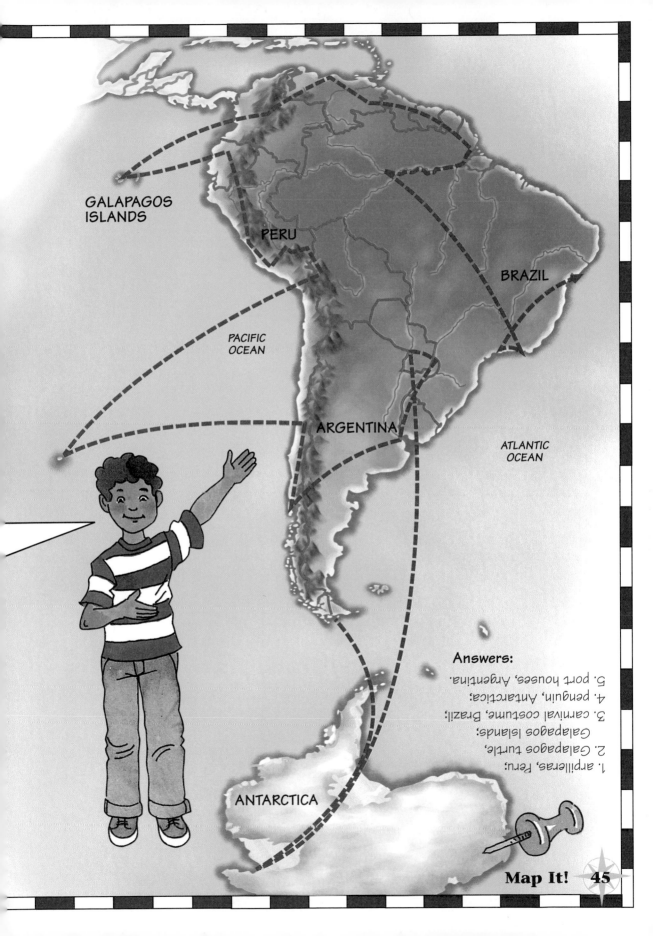

GALAPAGOS ISLANDS

PERU

BRAZIL

PACIFIC OCEAN

ARGENTINA

ATLANTIC OCEAN

ANTARCTICA

Answers:
1. arpilleras, Peru;
2. Galapagos turtle, Galapagos Islands;
3. carnival costume, Brazil;
4. penguin, Antarctica;
5. port houses, Argentina.

Map It! 45

Central America is the name for the group of countries at the southern tip of North America. On the north, Central America borders Mexico. On the south, it borders South America. The Pacific Ocean lies to the west. The Caribbean Sea, which is part of the Atlantic Ocean, lies to the east along with many islands. Rugged mountains crisscross Mexico and Central America. Many are active volcanoes. A chain of volcanoes forms a mountainous spine along the Pacific coast. It makes transportation difficult. It also makes it hard to develop businesses.

Where can you find the third largest pyramid in the world?

UNITED STATES

Gulf of Mexico

MEXICO

PACIFIC OCEAN

Mexico City

Mountains of Michoacán

February 26

We've travelled north but are still close to the equator. The Caribbean Sea is blue and warm. At the hotel, we learned that most of the Caribbean islands were created by volcanoes. Others are made of coral and limestone. Earthquakes and volcanic eruptions sometimes rock this region and cause a lot of damage, but we are safe right now.

Welcome to Central America and Mexico!

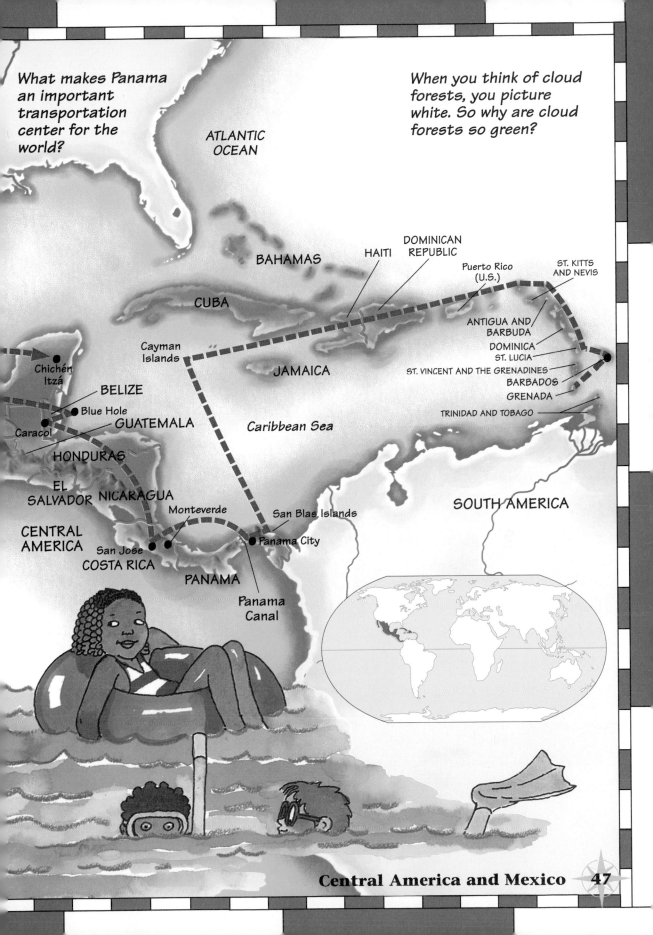

What makes Panama an important transportation center for the world?

When you think of cloud forests, you picture white. So why are cloud forests so green?

ATLANTIC OCEAN

BAHAMAS

HAITI

DOMINICAN REPUBLIC

Puerto Rico (U.S.)

ST. KITTS AND NEVIS

CUBA

ANTIGUA AND BARBUDA

DOMINICA

ST. LUCIA

Cayman Islands

JAMAICA

ST. VINCENT AND THE GRENADINES

BARBADOS

GRENADA

Chichén Itzá

BELIZE

Blue Hole

Caracol

GUATEMALA

TRINIDAD AND TOBAGO

Caribbean Sea

HONDURAS

EL SALVADOR

NICARAGUA

SOUTH AMERICA

Monteverde

San Blas Islands

CENTRAL AMERICA

San Jose

Panama City

COSTA RICA

PANAMA

Panama Canal

Central America and Mexico 47

February 27

Grenada's the place to find spices growing, and that's why it's called the "Spice Isle." The island's flag even has the fruit of the nutmeg tree on it. Nutmeg is an important crop in Grenada. Other spices, including cinnamon, cloves, pimento, and bay leaves, grow in the hills.

March 1

In the Caribbean Islands, meals are delightfully different from island to island. Here are some of the things we've tried.

In Grenada: Souse is a thick, rich stew of pig's feet that makes a hearty meal.

In Barbados: Flying fish and pickled breadfruit.

In Dominica: Mountain chicken drumsticks are delicious, but they come from a frog.

In Antigua: Goat water is a tender goat meat stewed in a spicy broth.

In Jamaica: Ackee may be our new favorite breakfast fruit. When it's cooked, it looks and tastes like scrambled eggs.

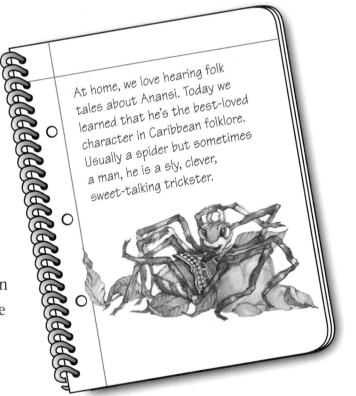

At home, we love hearing folk tales about Anansi. Today we learned that he's the best-loved character in Caribbean folklore. Usually a spider but sometimes a man, he is a sly, clever, sweet-talking trickster.

GUIDEBOOK/WEST INDIES

The British island of Montserrat is so unsafe right now that people can't even visit it. In 1989, Hurricane Hugo struck Montserrat. It severely damaged most of its buildings. Then in 1995, a volcano began a series of eruptions. Today the capital, Plymouth, is covered in rock and ash. All the people have left.

Welcome to the Cayman Islands

stingray

February 28

Dear Grandma,
On a boat trip off the Cayman Islands today, we saw stingrays! Their stingers are on their tails, and they'll sting if you hurt or frighten them. We dropped pieces of squid in the water and watched them eat.

Love,
Gabriel

March 3

Today we flew into Panama City, the capital
and largest city of Panama. The city lies at the
Pacific Ocean end of the Panama Canal. The
Panama Canal is a big waterway that
connects the Atlantic and Pacific oceans. Our
guide said that it almost didn't get built!
France began the canal, and the United States
finally completed it in 1914. We're sure
sailors were happy to see it open because it
made their voyage much shorter. They no
longer had to sail around South America.
What a difference! Panama is an important
transportation center, because thousands
of ships use the canal each year.

March 5

Julia thinks that from the airplane, the San Blas Islands
look like a bunch of stepping stones in the Atlantic
Ocean. There are about 365 islands, and the Cuna
people live on about 40 of them. No one lives on the
others. From a dugout canoe, we saw the beautiful
beaches of these islands. Then we spent the night with
a family in a house made of cane walls and covered
with a palm-thatched roof. There is no fresh water
supply on the islands, so the Cuna travel to the rivers
on the mainland of Panama to collect water each day.

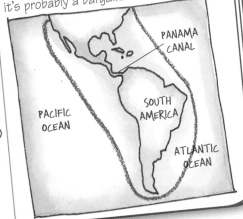

Ships passing through the Panama Canal pay around $35,000 for their eight-hour passage. That sounds like a lot. But if you think about how much it would cost in fuel, food, pay for workers, and time to travel all the way around South America, it's probably a bargain!

PANAMA CANAL

PACIFIC OCEAN

SOUTH AMERICA

ATLANTIC OCEAN

March 6

The Cuna men rise early to fish or farm on the mainland. They catch lobster, octopus, and fish with nets or spears. They sell their catch in Panama City. On farms, they grow vegetables, fruits, rice, and coconuts. We saw women making molas. They cut and stitch several layers of cloth to make patterns. Molas are used in the house or sewn on women's clothing.

San Blas Islands

Ma

Dear Grandma,
Today we saw women making molas, like on the front of this card. I also bought a soda with coconuts! Coconuts can be used as coins among the Cuna.

Love,
Steven

March 7

Our guidebook says that Costa Rica is the third smallest country of Central America. Today we flew into San Jose, the capital and largest city. From the airport, we passed by many hillsides planted with coffee trees. The coffee bean is called the *grano de oro* or "golden bean" here. San Jose is the center for trade in coffee, bananas, and sugar.

GUIDEBOOK/COSTA RICA

There could be no better name for Monteverde, which means "green mountain" in Spanish. This small Costa Rican town is home to Monteverde Cloud Forest Reserve, shown below. Cloud forests are unique to mountaintops. They are found in tropical and subtropical climates where clouds cling to the slopes and moisture forms on trees. The constant moisture allows for an incredible variety of plants and animals, including bugs!

March 8

At an open-air market, we bought postcards that show animals found in the Monteverde cloud forest.

Quetzal
Ancient Maya chiefs used the long tail feathers of this bird as a symbol of hospitality.

Monteverde, Costa Rica

Monteverde, Costa Rica

Golden Toad
This amphibian is thought to have disappeared from Monteverde, which was its only known home in the world.

Monteverde, Costa Rica

Ocelot
This member of the cat family is a great climber and hunts small animals.

March 9

A guide took us to Caracol, the largest known Maya ruin in Belize. She told us that Caracol has been found, lost, found, lost, and found again! The Maya Indians moved into this part of Central America hundreds of years ago. Caracol was an important place for them. The Spanish conquered almost all the Maya in the 1500's. Caracol was lost to the jungle. It was discovered in the 1930's, lost again, and then rediscovered in the 1950's. Because it was so hard to get to, it remained hidden and overgrown by jungle until the 1980's. Caracol is now being recovered from the jungle.

Caracol ruin

March 9

Dear Grandma,
Caves were important to the Maya Indians, but I'll bet they never went cave tubing! We rode rubber inner tubes into an underground river cave system. Our only light was our headlamps. We swirled around stalagmites and stalactites. Then we climbed into underground rooms where the Maya had carved altars, fireplaces, and statues of gods.

Love,
Julia

Blue Hole is exactly that, a deep, incredibly blue sinkhole. The hole started to form when the world was covered in ice a very long time ago. Because so much water was trapped in ice, the level of the sea sank. This exposed the limestone just off the coast of what is now Belize. As water flowed through the limestone, huge caves formed. When the ice melted, the sea level rose. The top that once covered the Blue Hole collapsed, leaving what we see today.

Rio Frio Caves

BELIZE

March 12

We'd heard about birds flying south for the winter, but we didn't know some butterflies do it, too! Each fall, monarch butterflies make their way to Mexico from Canada and the United States for the winter. When we got out of our tour bus in the mountains of Michoacán, we were surrounded by millions of them. Julia took some pictures. She said she felt like she was in the middle of an orange and black blizzard.

March 13

We're here in Mexico City, the capital of Mexico. This city is filled with history, culture—and people. It is one of the largest cities in the world. More than 23 million people live in and around the city. With so many people, there is not enough housing, safe drinking water, or transportation, and the traffic creates air pollution. But the city is also a center for business, and it's famous for art, dance, and fine museums.

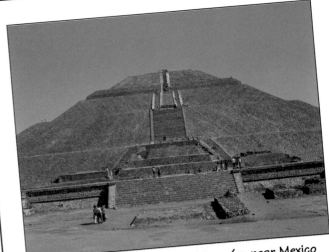

The Pyramid of the Sun at Teotihuacán, near Mexico City, is the third largest pyramid in the world.

March 14

Dear Grandpa,
Chichén Itzá was the most powerful city of the Maya Indians hundreds of years ago. Now something cool is about to happen here, as it's almost spring equinox. During the equinox, thanks to the sun, a serpent will appear to slither down the steps of the largest building, a pyramid called El Castillo. People come from all over to watch as the pyramid's stairs and a serpent-head carving are touched with sunlight, and the shadows appear to become a moving "serpent." The same thing happens on the fall equinox in September.

Love,
Yoshi

Chichén Itzá, Mexico

Mountains of Michoacán

Mexico City

Chichén Itzá

The United States covers the middle of North America. It stretches from the Atlantic Ocean in the east to the Pacific Ocean in the west. It also includes Alaska, in the northwest corner of North America; and Hawaii, far out in the Pacific. The land ranges from the warm beaches of Florida and Hawaii to the frozen lands of Alaska. People have settled just about everywhere. With so many different areas, the United States produces many kinds of farming products.

ALASKA (U.S.)

HAWAII (U.S.)

March 16

We've arrived in Miami, Florida. Parts of the city remind us of some of the places we visited in Central America, the Caribbean, and Mexico. The weather is warm; many tropical plants grow here, and many of Miami's people have come from neighboring countries. At our hotel, we watched a TV news report. It said that since 1959, hundreds of thousands of people have come to Miami from Cuba. In the late 1970's, many people from Haiti also began calling Miami home. Both groups have been coming to the United States because they don't like how the government runs their homeland.

Welcome to the United States!

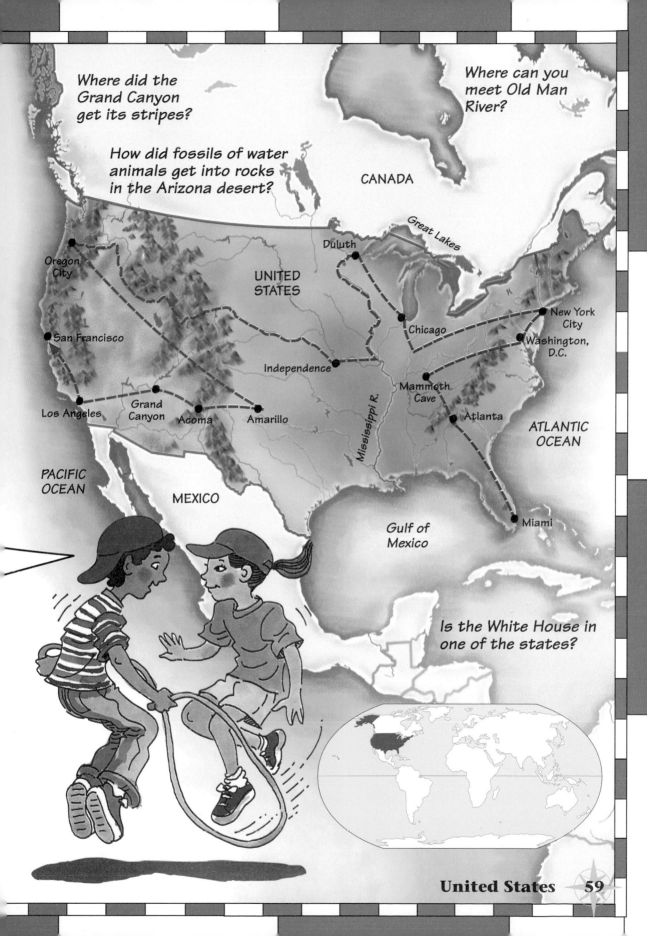

Where did the Grand Canyon get its stripes?

Where can you meet Old Man River?

How did fossils of water animals get into rocks in the Arizona desert?

CANADA

Great Lakes

Duluth

UNITED STATES

Oregon City

Chicago

New York City

Washington, D.C.

San Francisco

Independence

Mammoth Cave

Mississippi R.

Los Angeles

Grand Canyon

Acoma

Amarillo

Atlanta

ATLANTIC OCEAN

PACIFIC OCEAN

MEXICO

Gulf of Mexico

Miami

Is the White House in one of the states?

March 18

We took a walk through history today when we visited the city of Atlanta, in Georgia. The Martin Luther King, Jr., National Historic Site has Dr. King's birthplace, the church where he was minister, and the place where he was buried. A guide at the King Center told us that King inspired thousands of people to work for equal rights and protest the unfair treatment of black people. We heard a recording of the speech he gave in Washington, D.C., over 30 years ago. Yoshi said it made her feel as if we had been there with thousands of other people, listening to his words.

the tomb of Martin Luther King, Jr.

March 20

We toured a part of Mammoth Cave. It tunnels through underground layers of limestone in central Kentucky. We found out that the cave has formed over millions of years as water has trickled through cracks in the limestone and worn it away. We were surprised to see rocks of such awesome colors and shapes in the cave. They almost looked like flowers and trees.

Spelunking in Mammoth Cave!

March 24

Walking around Ellis Island in New York Harbor, you can imagine that you're coming to the United States to find a better life. We could almost feel the hope—and the fear of the unknown. Audiotape recordings at the Ellis Island Immigration Museum tell how more than 12 million people from all over the world entered the United States through Ellis Island. They were checked by doctors and asked questions before beginning their new life. We also visited the Statue of Liberty, a majestic sculpture that stands at the entrance to New York Harbor. It must have been the first thing many people saw when they came here.

March 22

Dear Grandma,
Today we're not in any state. We're in Washington, D.C., the capital of the United States. It's in an area called the District of Columbia. We just toured the White House, where the President lives. It's a mansion, filled with United States history!

Love,
Yoshi

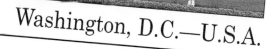
Washington, D.C.—U.S.A.

United States 61

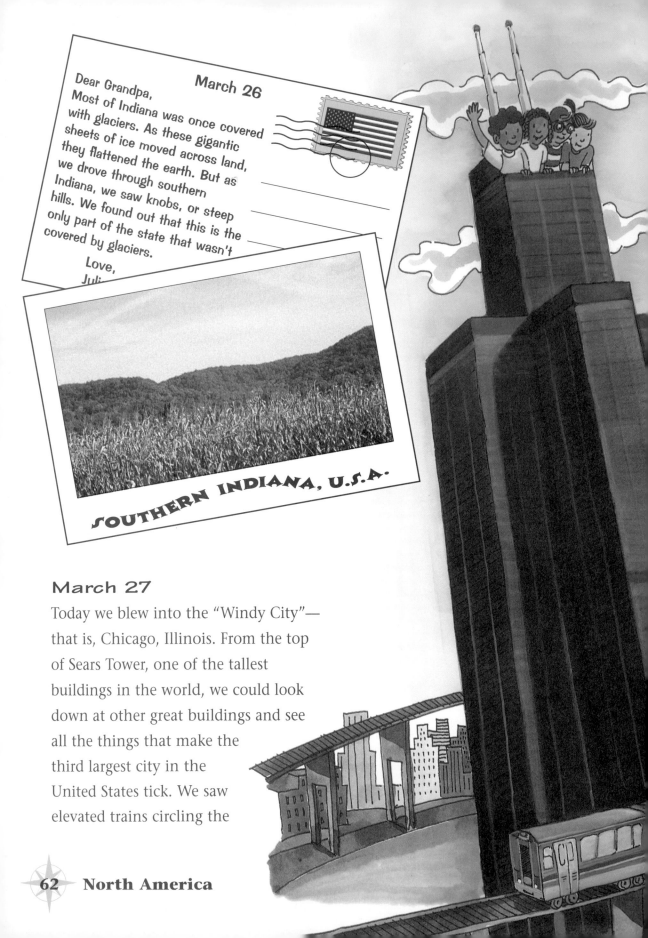

Dear Grandpa,
Most of Indiana was once covered with glaciers. As these gigantic sheets of ice moved across land, they flattened the earth. But as we drove through southern Indiana, we saw knobs, or steep hills. We found out that this is the only part of the state that wasn't covered by glaciers.

Love,
Juli

March 26

SOUTHERN INDIANA, U.S.A.

March 27

Today we blew into the "Windy City"—that is, Chicago, Illinois. From the top of Sears Tower, one of the tallest buildings in the world, we could look down at other great buildings and see all the things that make the third largest city in the United States tick. We saw elevated trains circling the city. We watched boats go up and down the Chicago River, and we admired the Lake Michigan shoreline.

March 29

"Old Man River" is a pretty neat nickname. That's what some people call the Mississippi River. We found out that Old Man River is the second longest river in the United States, after the Missouri River. It begins in the state of Minnesota and flows southward all the way down the country to the Gulf of Mexico. No wonder it has been so important to the history of the United States.

During the 1500's and 1600's, Spanish and French explorers traveled down the river in search of land to call their own. When steamboats were invented in the 1800's, the river became a great transportation and trade route. Mark Twain wrote about the Mississippi in the days when great paddle-wheeled steamboats carried passengers and cargo up and down the river.

In Duluth, Minnesota, we saw Lake Superior. Like Lake Michigan, it's one of the five Great Lakes. A fisherman told us that the Great Lakes are the most important inland waterway in North America and the largest group of freshwater lakes in the world. Early explorers and settlers used them for travel. Later, industries grew up in the area.

GREAT LAKES

Superior

Huron

Ontario

Duluth

Michigan

Chicago

Erie

April 1

Talk about living history! We're going to follow the same path that thousands of people trekked as they moved west to Oregon in the 1800's. We'll start in Independence, Missouri, just as the settlers did. We plan to go all the way to Oregon City, Oregon.

April 3

Boy, those settlers on the Oregon Trail had to have been tired of traveling! Each day was exactly the same: break camp, walk and walk and walk, and then make camp again. We couldn't understand why they didn't just ride in their wagons. Our guidebook said that they walked to spare the oxen or mules pulling the wagons from having to pull the extra weight. So there they were, in a cloud of dust and grit thrown up by the wagons and animals. Yuck! When they weren't doing that, they were crossing a dangerous river or climbing a steep hill. Could we have made it to Oregon if we took this trip back then?

Oregon City

OREGON

Disease Travels, Too

Most Indians welcomed their new neighbors along the Oregon Trail. They saw them as a source of wealth, because they could trade for food, clothes, or horses that the settlers brought. But the settlers also brought smallpox, measles, and other diseases that killed whole tribes of Indians and many white settlers.

April 5

Traveling the Oregon Trail sounds so exciting. People usually traveled in groups of wagons, known as wagon trains. The trail was often crowded. There were even sightseeing tours! Most of the travelers went about 20 miles each day. Some people left their heavier belongings, such as iron stoves, along the trail because they became too difficult to carry. In the 1840's, married settlers could claim an area of land in the Oregon Country for free.

Independence

MISSOURI

An Indian welcomes a settler.

April 6

We made it to Oregon. What took us just a few days, took the settlers up to six months! We can't even imagine how hard that must have been.

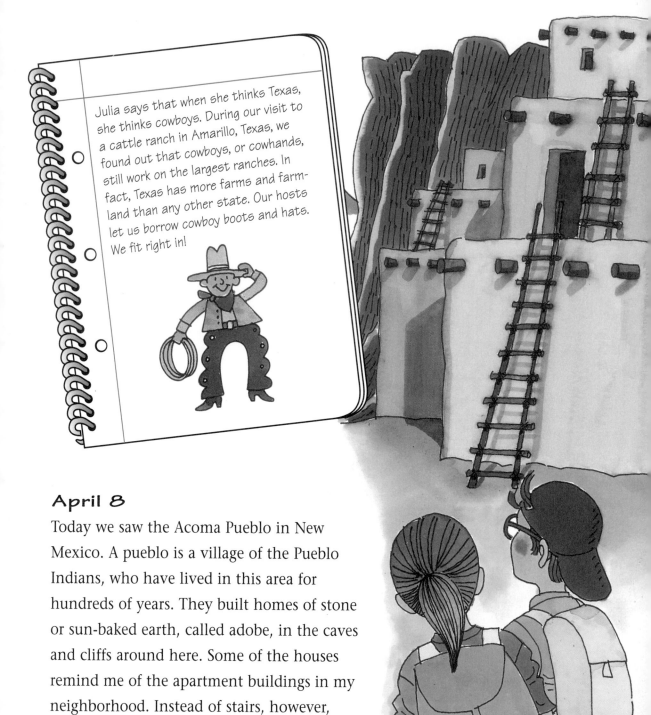

Julia says that when she thinks Texas, she thinks cowboys. During our visit to a cattle ranch in Amarillo, Texas, we found out that cowboys, or cowhands, still work on the largest ranches. In fact, Texas has more farms and farmland than any other state. Our hosts let us borrow cowboy boots and hats. We fit right in!

April 8

Today we saw the Acoma Pueblo in New Mexico. A pueblo is a village of the Pueblo Indians, who have lived in this area for hundreds of years. They built homes of stone or sun-baked earth, called adobe, in the caves and cliffs around here. Some of the houses remind me of the apartment buildings in my neighborhood. Instead of stairs, however, people use ladders to climb up or down.

April 9

We couldn't wait to get to Arizona to see the Grand Canyon. It was as incredible as we expected. The colors were awesome! Our tour guide explained that the different colors show different layers of rock. Yoshi asked her how the layers got there. Our guide said that at two different times very tall mountains stood where the Grand Canyon is today. Over millions of years, the mountains eroded, or wore away, to form an area of level land. At times when the land became lower, the ocean moved in and covered it. The ocean moved back and forth over this land many times in its history. Each time this happened, a new layer of rock was left behind.

Then the Colorado River came into the picture. The river formed the canyon over millions of years by cutting through the layers of rock. The river exposed all these layers as it carved its path. That's how we can see the rocks in all their many colors today.

the Grand Canyon and its many layers of rock

GUIDEBOOK/UNITED STATES

Fossils are the remains of plants or animals that lived long ago. They are usually found in rock. Fossils found in the Grand Canyon walls tell scientists that animals and plants lived there millions of years ago. Many fossils are those of creatures that lived in the ocean. They help prove that the ocean covered the area at different times.

amphibian track fossils

April 11

We spent the last two days star-gazing. No, not at the kind in the sky, but at movie stars! Los Angeles, its Hollywood area in particular, is famous for its movies and TV shows. Lots of actors and actresses work here. Los Angeles is a glamorous city with some beautiful homes. But the city also has problems. Millions of people live here. There is little open land left, and housing is in short supply. Also, most people use cars for transportation. The freeways are jammed, and fumes from the cars and smoke from factories have created serious air pollution. One way the city is working to solve this problem is with a better public transportation system. We rode around on buses as much as we could.

April 12

The Golden Gate Bridge, clanging cable cars, hills—all of these say San Francisco. My favorite part of this California city was Chinatown. We found out that it's one of the largest Chinese communities outside Asia, with about 130,000 people of Chinese ancestry. Our waiter said that many Chinese came here to work in the mines during the gold rush of 1849. Thousands more arrived in the 1860's to help build railroads. We saw an ad for an apothecary, a person who prepares and sells medicine, like a pharmacist.

San Francisco

California

Visit Mr. Liu
Apothecary and Acupuncturist

Located in the heart of Chinatown, I specialize in traditional Chinese medicine, which has been used for hundreds of years. I offer acupuncture, an ancient method of relieving pain and treating disease by inserting needles into specific places on the body. I am also an apothecary. I make and sell Chinese herbal medicines. Different herbs are known to work together to improve your health. The goal of Chinese herbal therapy is to balance the life energy, or chi. Stop in and see what Chinese medicine can do for you.

SAN FRANCISCO

April 12

Dear Grandma,
Doesn't it look like this postcard is from China? It's actually Chinatown in San Francisco. Many of the buildings here are topped with Chinese-style upturned roofs.

Love,
Julia

Los Angeles

Canada stretches from the Atlantic Ocean in the east to the Pacific in the west. Its northernmost parts are vast, cold lands of the Arctic. In the south, it borders the United States. Canada is the second largest country in the world. Even so, the United States, which is smaller, has 10 times more people. Parts of Canada are very cold or very wild and rugged, and not many people live in those areas. Canada is made up of 10 provinces, which are like states, and three territories.

Canada is a land of great beauty, with towering mountains, thick forests, sparkling lakes, rushing rivers, and a long coastline. It is also rich in natural resources, such as lumber and farmland, as well as minerals such as oil and iron ore.

You just have to visit the Polar Bear Capital of the World. Where is it?

ARCTIC OCEAN

ALASKA (U.S.)

Dawson

PACIFIC OCEAN

Yoho National Park

Calgary

Victoria

Vancouver

Welcome to Canada!

April 13

We've just crossed the border from Washington state into the province of British Columbia, Canada. Even though Alaska is a state in the United States, we are closer to it in Canada than we ever were in the U.S.A. That's because Alaska borders Canada, not the United States. That's something we never thought about before!

Why was April 1, 1999, such an important date for the Inuit?

Greenland (Denmark)

Why is "Yoho" a good name for a national park?

Why do some people in Canada speak English and some speak French?

Yellowknife

Hudson Bay

Churchill

Newfoundland

Wood Buffalo National Park

Churchill River

CANADA

Regina

Prince Edward Island

St. Lawrence River

St. John River

Bay of Fundy

Great Lakes

Montreal

Grand Manan Island

UNITED STATES

Toronto

Niagara Falls

ATLANTIC OCEAN

April 13

Victoria, the capital of the province of British Columbia, is our first stop in Canada. We are still so close to the United States. We spent a whole afternoon studying the totally cool totem poles at the Royal British Columbia Museum. Totem poles were wood carvings made by American Indians. Many tribes carved the family and clan emblems on totem poles.

April 15

We rode a ferry from Victoria to Vancouver, about an hour-and-a-half journey. Once in Vancouver, we headed north to the Capilano Suspension Bridge, which crosses over the Capilano River. It spans 450 feet. We were all a little uneasy walking over the bridge because it swayed and creaked. Our guide assured us, however, that the bridge is very, very strong—strong enough to support the weight of 10 heavy-duty military planes. That wasn't good enough for Steven. He wanted to get off the bridge as soon as possible. Unfortunately, we had to cross the bridge again to get back to our bus!

April 17

We visited a fossil-filled area of Yoho National Park. Yoshi looked up information about fossils. She says that if it hadn't been for the "Cambrian Explosion," fossil hunters wouldn't have much to look at. For about 3 billion years, only simple living things existed on the earth. Then, during a time called the Cambrian Period, many complex types of animals appeared in the oceans in just a few million years. That sounds like a long time, but compared to billions of years, it's not very long at all!

PHRASE BOOK

The name "Yoho" also is given to a river, a mountain, a glacier, and a pass. It is usually connected with a word that Cree Indians use to express wonder or excitement.

April 19

We made it to Calgary, the largest city in the province of Alberta. Calgary is located in the foothills of the Canadian Rocky Mountains. It also lies at the junction of the Bow and Elbow rivers. Both rivers run right through the city. Its location has made Calgary a major transportation and distribution center.

April 20

Everyone else was awed by the cadets who were training to be Royal Canadian Mounted Police, but Gabe was crazy about the horses. We saw them at the training center in Regina, Saskatchewan. In the Royal Canadian Mounted Police Centennial Museum next door, we saw the uniforms the cadets will wear when they get to be officers—scarlet red coats and wide-brimmed hats.

We learned that in the 1870's, outlaws in the western plains were causing trouble. So Canada's prime minister formed the first police force, the North West Mounted Police. In 1874, officers on horses set out to bring peace to Canada's prairies. That was the beginning of the Mounted Police. Today they are the national law enforcement department of Canada. They travel in cars, but they still use horses in ceremonies and demonstrations.

April 21

Dear Dad,
Today we saw a real polar bear in Churchill, Manitoba, the "polar bear capital of the world"! In the fall, the great white bears move through this area and out onto the ice of Hudson Bay to live. That's the best time to see them. In the spring, they return this way. Our guide said we might spot one—and we did. Can we come back next fall, please?!!

Love,
Steven

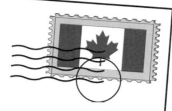

Churchill, Manitoba

Name the Foal Contest!

The Royal Canadian Mounted Police will have four beautiful new foals, or baby horses, this spring, and children will get to help name them. Each child should suggest one name. It should start with the letter R, as in Royal, and be no longer than six letters. Enter your idea today!

April 22

Buffalo are such awesome animals! We visited Wood Buffalo National Park and saw some of these magnificent creatures in the flesh. The park, mostly in Alberta and partly in the Northwest Territories, is Canada's largest national park and one of the largest in the world. A ranger told us that the park was established in 1922 to protect the last wood buffalo herds of the area.

April 23

To learn about the gold rush in Canada, we went to Dawson in the Yukon Territory. People there said the town looks just as it did when gold was discovered in 1896. We found out about the gold rush at the Dawson City Museum. Then we drove to Bonanza Creek, where gold is still mined. The creek was still frozen, but a man who rents out mining equipment told us that in a month or so, the ice would be gone and we could pan for gold. Julia wants to come back and look for it.

April 24

Yellowknife is the biggest town in the Northwest Territories. The land here is huge! Towns are so far apart that we fly in a small airplane wherever we go. Because we're so far north, the days are getting very long as summer approaches. It's weird going to bed while the sun is still shining! It's so beautiful, though.

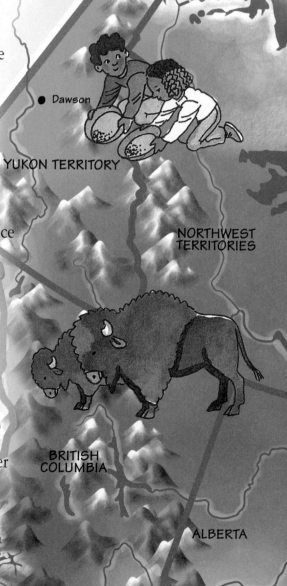

Dawson

YUKON TERRITORY

NORTHWEST TERRITORIES

BRITISH COLUMBIA

ALBERTA

The Wild North

The eastern part of the Northwest Territories became Nunavut, a separate territory of Canada, on April 1, 1999. The name means "Our Land" in the language of the Inuit, the native people of this area of Canada. Now the Inuit, who have lived here for thousands of years, once again have a land to call their own.

Two men raise the Nunavut flag.

NUNAVUT

●Yellowknife

Wood Buffalo National Park

SASKATCHEWAN

Wood Buffalo National Park is the last remaining nesting area for the endangered whooping crane. The cranes nest in the remote north-central area of the park. It is a watery place of marshes, shallow ponds and lakes, streams, and bogs.

April 27

We didn't want to miss Niagara Falls—especially Yoshi. Her grandparents came here after they got married. But they visited the New York side. We're on the Ontario side. You see, Niagara Falls is actually two waterfalls, the Horseshoe Falls and the American Falls.

April 29

Oui, Oui (that's French for "yes, yes"), Montreal is very French. In fact, French is the official language of Quebec, the province where Montreal is located. About half of the people in Montreal speak both English and French. Some people speak only French, and most schools teach in French.

ONTARIO

Lake Superior

Lake Huron

Lake Michigan

"Old Montreal" is a charming area of the city.

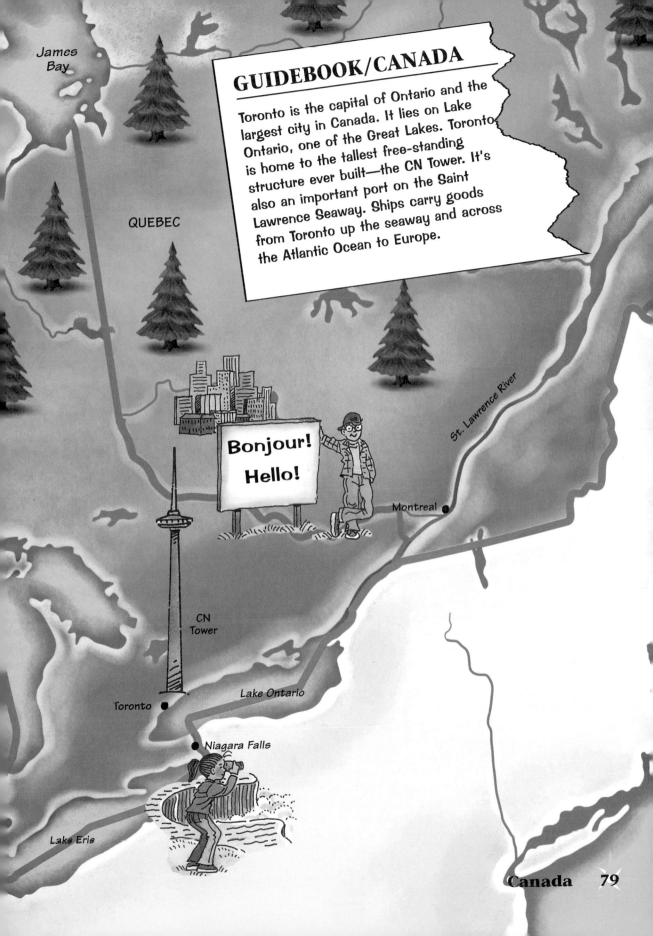

James Bay

QUEBEC

GUIDEBOOK/CANADA

Toronto is the capital of Ontario and the largest city in Canada. It lies on Lake Ontario, one of the Great Lakes. Toronto is home to the tallest free-standing structure ever built—the CN Tower. It's also an important port on the Saint Lawrence Seaway. Ships carry goods from Toronto up the seaway and across the Atlantic Ocean to Europe.

St. Lawrence River

Bonjour!

Hello!

Montreal

CN Tower

Lake Ontario

Toronto

Niagara Falls

Lake Erie

May 1

Dear Grandma,
Today we saw the Reversing Falls of the Saint John River in the province of New Brunswick. We watched as the tide rushed in and made the river flow backward up over the waterfall. Later, we drove to The Rocks provincial park and saw the flowerpot rocks. They're big rocks with trees growing from the tops. When the tide is in, the rocks are in the water.

Love,
Julia

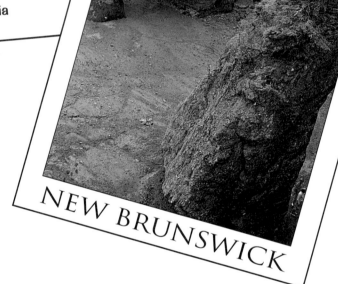

NEW BRUNSWICK

May 3

We rode a ferry to Grand Manan Island in the Bay of Fundy. Guess what we ate—seaweed! It's called dulse, and we picked it on the shore and dried it in the sun before we ate it. It was tasty. Farther along the shore, we saw all kinds of seals and even a few early puffins and other birds. Later this month there will be thousands!

GUIDEBOOK/CANADA

The Bay of Fundy has the highest tides in the world. The Reversing Falls is a result of these amazing tides. At low tide, the bay drops below the level of the river. The river water rushes through the narrow riverbed and over a rock barrier toward the bay. At high tide, the bay water rushes back up the riverbed and over the rocks—a backward waterfall!

seals basking on Grand Manan Island

May 5

We arrived in Prince Edward Island today. The people here call it P. E. I. We went to the Green Gables House—the green-and-white home of Anne, the main character in *Anne of Green Gables,* Yoshi's and Julia's favorite book of all time. We walked all through the house and around the grounds and explored the places they had read about in the book. We felt as though we were Anne!

MAP IT!
North America

Hudson Bay

CANADA

ATLANTIC OCEAN

UNITED STATES

PACIFIC OCEAN

CARIBBEAN ISLANDS

Gulf of Mexico

MEXICO

Caribbean Sea

Answers:
1. mola, Panama;
2. totem pole, Canada;
3. Anansi, Caribbean Islands;
4. White House, United States;
5. Chichén Itzá, Mexico.

PANAMA

We did it. We traveled all the way across another continent—North America. See the giant thumbtacks on this page? Inside each one is a picture clue of one of our favorite places in North America. If the thumbtacks were real, could you pin each one correctly on the map to show in which country the pictured place is? We drew the route to remind you of where our travels took us.

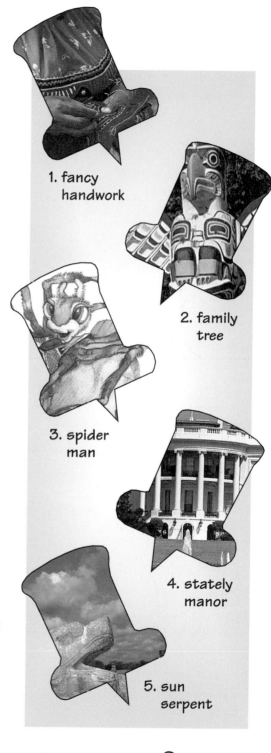

1. fancy handwork

2. family tree

3. spider man

4. stately manor

5. sun serpent

Western Europe stretches from the Atlantic Ocean to Asia, from north of the Arctic Circle to the Mediterranean Sea. The climate here ranges from the frigid cold of northern Norway, Sweden, and Finland to the sun-baked beaches of Spain, to the windy, wet shores of Ireland, to the snowy mountaintops of Austria and Switzerland. Western Europe is a place of tremendous beauty and rich history.

May 6

After sleeping on our overnight flight from Halifax to Dublin, the capital of the Republic of Ireland, we were ready to go. Ireland is damp, rainy, but oh-so-lush and green! We bicycled to a cozy shop to start our day with tea and warm biscuits called scones.

Welcome to Western Europe!

How were the Alps formed?

Who is the Sun King?

Why are there canals instead of streets in Venice?

How did Beefeaters get their name?

Lapland

Rovaniemi

ICELAND
Reykjavik

FINLAND

SWEDEN

Helsinki

NORWAY

ESTONIA

Oslo

Stockholm

LATVIA

Kristiansand

LITHUANIA

ATLANTIC OCEAN

North Sea

DENMARK

Baltic Sea

Silkeborg

Edinburgh

Lake District

Billund

Copenhagen

IRELAND

Dublin

Snowdonia National Park

NETHERLANDS

POLAND

UNITED KINGDOM

Edam

Berlin

Gravesend

Amsterdam

GERMANY

London

Brussels

CZECH REPUBLIC

English Channel

BELGIUM

Rhine River

SLOVAKIA

Seine River

Paris

LUXEMBOURG

Danube River

Vienna

Versailles

Munich

HUNGARY

Loire River

FRANCE

AUSTRIA

SWITZERLAND

ALPS

SLOVENIA

CROATIA

Venice

BOSNIA-HERZEGOVINA

Po River

Ebro River

Duero River

ITALY

Madrid

Rome

PORTUGAL

Tagus River

Naples

Lisbon

Cuenca

Tyrrhenian Sea

SPAIN

Mediterranean Sea

May 7

Today, we headed straight to Phoenix Park beside the River Liffey in Dublin. It's the largest city park in Europe. We watched a game of hurling there. Players raced up and down a field, using wooden sticks to whip a small, hard ball around. Hurling looks like lacrosse and field hockey combined. It's been played in Ireland for over 2,000 years!

May 8

A short plane ride and we're in the United Kingdom, also called Britain. This country is made up of Northern Ireland, Scotland, Wales, and England. In Scotland, we walked Edinburgh's Royal Mile to Holyroodhouse Palace, where the British royal family stays when they visit. We passed bagpipe makers, kilt makers, weavers, pubs, and kirks (churches). Steven loved the royal Holyrood Park. You can stroll like royalty, climb the hills, or sit and watch at the park's bird sanctuary.

Shetland Islands

Orkney Islands

North Sea

Loch Ness

Scotland

ATLANTIC OCEAN

Glasgow
Clyde River
Edinburgh

UNITED

KINGDOM

Newcastle upon Tyne

Northern Ireland

Belfast

Lake District

Irish Sea

Leeds

IRELAND

Shannon River

Dublin

River Liffey

Llanfairpwllgwyngyll

Manchester
Liverpool
Sheffield

Snowdon

England

Birmingham

Wales

Severn River

Cardiff

Thames River

Bristol

English Channel

Land's End

GUIDEBOOK/IRELAND

The Book of Kells at Trinity College in Dublin is one of the world's most beautiful books. This manuscript was created by monks in Ireland more than 1,000 years ago. The pages are lettered by hand. They are decorated with colorful designs that wind around human figures and animals.

May 10

CROESO I CYMRU! That means "WELCOME TO WALES!" Today we're at Snowdonia National Park in northern Wales, where the mountains are beautiful! These mountains were once known for coal, slate, and gold mining, and they're great for climbing. We took the Snowdon Mountain Railway right to the top of the highest mountain in Wales, the 3,561-foot Snowdon Peak. From there, we could see from Wales to England and Ireland.

May 11

Llanfairpwllgwyngyllgogerychwyrndrobwllllan-tysiliogogogoch. Our guide wrote down the word and told us that a town in Wales used to be called by that name. It meant "Church of Saint Mary in the hollow of the white hazel near a rapid whirlpool and Saint Tysilio near the red cave." Now the town is just called Llanfairpwllgwyngyll.

In Welsh, Snowdon is called Yr Wyddfa, which means "tomb." It is said to be the burial place of a giant who wore a coat made from the beards of kings he had killed. Who killed him? King Arthur himself!

Humber River

London
Gravesend
Dover
Folkestone
Chunnel
Calais
FRANCE

Peter Rabbit

May 12

We were in the neighborhood of an old friend today—Peter Rabbit! We were driving around the Lake District in northwestern England. We discovered that Beatrix Potter wrote and illustrated her stories here. At the old stone farmhouse where she lived, we saw relatives of her famous characters hopping, waddling, and meowing! Later, we looked at some of her drawings. Here's a picture of Peter getting into trouble!

May 13

When Julia heard that Pocahontas was buried at Gravesend, England, she begged to come here. She told us that Pocahontas was an Indian girl who helped her people and the English settlers live in peace. She married settler John Rolfe. In 1616, they visited England with their son. In England, Pocahontas was treated like a princess, but before they could return to America, she died of smallpox and is buried here. We saw a beautiful picture of her that was painted shortly before her death.

Derwentwater in the Lake District, England

We also found out where time begins—in Greenwich, London. The 0° longitude line on a map is the north-south line that passes through Greenwich, a borough, or area, of the city. Lines of longitude are counted east and west from here. The world's 24 time zones start ticking in Greenwich. As you go east, each zone is one hour later. As you go west, each zone is one hour earlier.

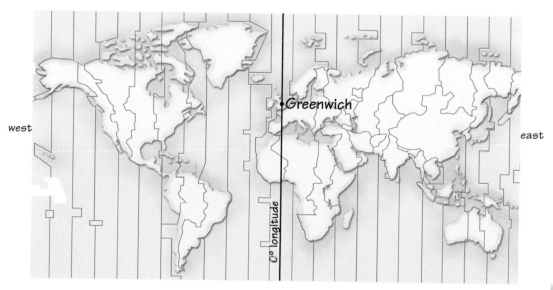

May 14

"Off to the Tower with you!" When an English king or queen said that, you were bound to be locked up in the Tower of London, and maybe beheaded! The Tower of London was once a fortress. King after king added to it until it became like a small town surrounded by thick stone walls. The Tower has been a fort, a royal palace, a prison, and an execution site. The oldest building is the White Tower. We visited the Tower with a group from a British school. We saw the Crown Jewels and got to try on replicas of them. We put on real armor, too.

We learned that at least least six ravens always live at the Tower. They are very well cared for, and their wings are clipped so they can't fly away. A legend says that if the ravens leave the Tower of London, the White Tower would crumble and a great disaster would happen to the kingdom.

the Tower of London on the Thames River

GUIDEBOOK/UNITED KINGDOM

The royal guard of the Tower are the Yeoman Warders, but since the 1670's they've been called Beefeaters. Why? Some people say it's because they once got part of their pay in meat! Others say it is because long ago, they tested the king's food for poison before he ate it.

the palace of Versailles and one of its gardens

May 16

Magnificent! We just visited Versailles, the palace of Louis XIV. In French, you pronounce his name LOO ee, but he liked to be called "Le roi-soleil," meaning "The Sun King." Louis XIV was king for 72 years. When he ruled, France was first in art, literature, war, and just about everything else!

Versailles took more than 40 years to build. It is over 1/4 mile long and has about 1,300 rooms. Louis XIV sat on solid silver furniture and dined on gold or silver dishes. Dozens of gentlemen attended the king's formal *levee* (getting up) and *coucher* (going to bed). People who visited him at court, where he lived, had to stand before him. For the royal family, there were rules about who could sit in an armchair, a regular chair, or a stool.

a room at Versailles with a magnificent fireplace

Poire Helene

Pears are an important crop in France. We couldn't leave without a tasty sample. This French recipe for Poire Helene (Pears Helen) is a keeper!

- Put 2 spoonfuls of chocolate syrup, then 1 scoop of ice cream in each person's bowl.
- Top each scoop of ice cream with half a canned pear.
- Mix 8 tablespoons jam and 1 tablespoon warm water in a small bowl.
- Spoon a little jam mixture over the pears and serve.

May 16

Dear Dad,
What a trip! We just rode a high-speed train through the "Chunnel," the tunnel that goes under the English Channel from Folkestone, England, to Coquelles, France. Then we rode the Paris Metro, the underground train. It took us to the Cathedral of Notre Dame, the Arc de Triomphe, the Eiffel Tower, and the Louvre.

Love,
Julia

Eiffel Tower

Paris, France

Arc de Triomphe

Paris, France

The balconies of the Hanging Houses at Cuenca, Spain, offer a breathtaking view— straight down!

May 18

We found out that Portugal and Spain provide most of the world's cork. Today we watched men strip long pieces of cork bark from cork oak trees. They said cork trees live 300 to 400 years. Each tree can be stripped only once every 8 to 10 years. Amazing!

May 20

We're still shaking! We ate lunch suspended over the deep gorge of the Huecar River! Lunch was great, and the view was even better. We were in a restaurant in the famous Hanging Houses (Las

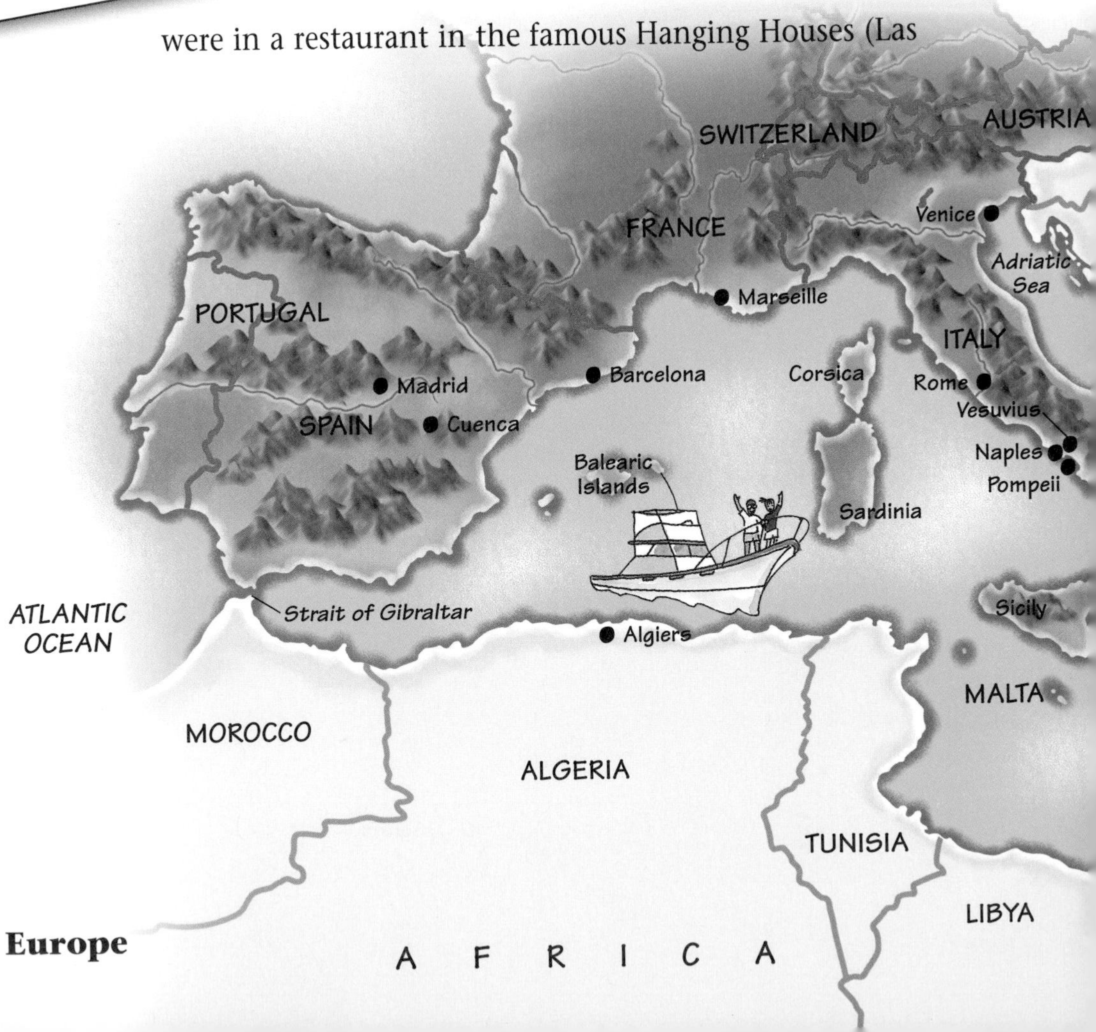

SWITZERLAND
AUSTRIA
FRANCE
Venice
Adriatic Sea
PORTUGAL
Marseille
ITALY
Madrid
Barcelona
Corsica
Rome
Vesuvius
SPAIN
Cuenca
Naples
Balearic Islands
Pompeii
Sardinia
ATLANTIC OCEAN
Strait of Gibraltar
Sicily
Algiers
MALTA
MOROCCO
ALGERIA
TUNISIA
LIBYA

A F R I C A

Casas Colgadas) in Cuenca, about 90 miles south of Madrid. Hundreds of years ago, the stone and cement houses were built out from the rock cliffs above the gorge. Their porches stick out from the houses—over thin air.

May 22

We arrived in Naples, Italy, on a ship from Spain. Sailing across the Mediterranean Sea felt like voyaging back through history. The ship's captain said the Mediterranean Sea has been one of the most important

GUIDEBOOK/PORTUGAL

Henry the Navigator—This Portuguese prince did not earn his nickname by sailing a ship. He brought together mapmakers, astronomers, and mathematicians from all over. He also sent out more than 50 groups of explorers during the 1400's. He made Portugal a world leader in seafaring exploration.

trade routes since ancient times. My map showed why. The Mediterranean touches Europe on the north, Asia on the east, Africa on the south, and the Atlantic Ocean on the west.

MACEDONIA   Istanbul

ALBANIA

GREECE   Aegean Sea

A S I A

TURKEY

Athens

SYRIA

CYPRUS

Crete   LEBANON

M e d i t e r r a n e a n   S e a   ISRAEL

JORDAN

EGYPT   Nile River   Cairo

May 24

Rome is called the Eternal City because it's been a major city for thousands of years. We call it that because we'd like to explore here forever! We've seen the Colosseum where ancient Romans watched gladiators battle wild animals. We also saw the ruins of part of the largest Roman baths, where 3,000 people could bathe at one time, and the Pantheon, a temple early Romans built to honor their gods. The ancient city was built on seven hills. We must have walked up and down every one!

The Colosseum, an ancient Roman stadium, could seat about 50,000 people.

The Pantheon was built to honor many Roman gods. It is still in almost perfect condition.

We found out that the Bridge of Sighs in Venice got its name because unhappy prisoners crossed it one way to go to trial, the other to go to prison or be executed.

May 26

We rode in a gondola—a skinny boat—through the streets of Venice. Most of the streets here are canals because Venice actually is built on a group of islands in the Adriatic Sea. There are more than 150 canals, more than 400 bridges, and such incredible buildings surrounded by water! People are working to fix up buildings, paintings, and statues that have been damaged by floods and pollution. We sat and ate gelato, Italian ice cream, counting all the bridges that we walked across today.

GUIDEBOOK/ITALY

Near Naples, visit the "lost city" of Pompeii. Nearly 2,000 years ago, the volcano Mount Vesuvius erupted violently, quickly burying Pompeii and nearby Herculaneum. For hundreds of years, the city and more than 2,000 victims remained buried under layers of ash and lava. Today, you can walk through the parts of the city that have been dug up and see plaster molds of the people lying exactly as they were when they died and were trapped by falling ash.

May 29

Today, we saw the best of the best of horse riding in Vienna, Austria. At the Spanish Riding School of Vienna (Spanische Reitschule), we watched the Lipizzaner horses perform.

What a show! The horses danced under chandeliers to music by the world-famous composer Mozart. We learned that the Lipizzaners are descended from horses that came from Spain and Italy. They are all white, but are born black, brown, or gray and turn white as they grow up.

June 1

In Munich, Germany, we watched the Rathaus (city hall) clock tower's glockenspiel mark the time in a big, big way. On one level, full-sized figures in Bavarian dress dance by. Above them, musicians and clowns entertain the nobles. We wanted to see it again later that day, but we had to move on.

June 3

Looking at the highest peaks of the snow-capped Alps rising more than 15,000 ft. in the air, it's hard to realize that 100 million years ago, these mountains were the flat bottom of a huge sea. We learned that land masses from the north and south moved toward each other, folding the seabed into ridges and valleys and pushing it up and up. Yoshi thinks maybe we could find fish fossils in the limestone on some of those peaks!

DENMARK

North Sea

Hamburg

Elbe River

Weser River

NETHERLANDS

GERMANY

Rhine River

BELGIUM

Cologne

Frankfurt

LUXEMBOURG

Main River

FRANCE

Rhine River

Danube River

Bavaria

Munich

Zurich

SWITZERLAND

Bern

LIECHTENSTEIN

Geneva

Alps

Po River

ITALY

Baltic
Sea

POLAND

● Berlin

Oder River

CZECH
REPUBLIC

SLOVAKIA

Vienna ●

Danube River

AUSTRIA

HUNGARY

SLOVENIA

CROATIA

Adriatic
Sea

The glockenspiel on the city hall in Munich has figures that move to mark the time.

May 29

Dear Grandma,
Yum! We could eat our way across Europe! We stopped in a konditorei— a pastry shop—in Vienna. Our favorite sample was of sachertorte, a chocolate cake with layers of apricot jam.

Love,
Julia

A Konditorei, Vienna

Western Europe   99

GUIDEBOOK/SWITZERLAND

The Rhine River, more than 800 miles (1,287 kilometers) long, is the main inland waterway of Europe. It borders parts of Switzerland, Liechtenstein, Austria, France, and Germany, and flows through Germany and the Netherlands to the North Sea. Along its banks are castles built in the Middle Ages, when European countries were often at war.

North Sea

Edam
Amsterdam

Leiden

NETHERLANDS

BELGIUM

Rhine River

GERMANY

FRANCE

LIECHTENSTEIN

AUSTRIA

SWITZERLAND

June 6

Today, we got to see—and sample—how Edam cheese is made. At an outdoor stall in Edam, we each picked a little ball of hard cheese, called a "round." Each one is wrapped in a wax shell to keep it fresh. We sat in the grass and feasted on slices of Edam with bread. Tasty!

June 8

This morning we visited the world's largest flower market in Aalsmeer, near Amsterdam in the Netherlands. Millions of cut flowers and plants are auctioned off here every day and then shipped all over the world. Roses, tulips, and chrysanthemums are the favorites. Most of the flowers are grown here in the Netherlands.

Flowers and plants grown in these tulip fields near Leiden are shipped all over the world.

As we traveled through the Netherlands, we watched for stopped windmills. According to our guidebook, the owner stops the sails in a certain direction to say something. This is what we saw and read:

1. Top sail at 1 o'clock means "good news."
2. Top sail at 12 o'clock means "the mill is resting for a short time."
3. Top sail at 11 o'clock means "there's been a death."
4. Sails forming an X means "the mill is resting for a long time."

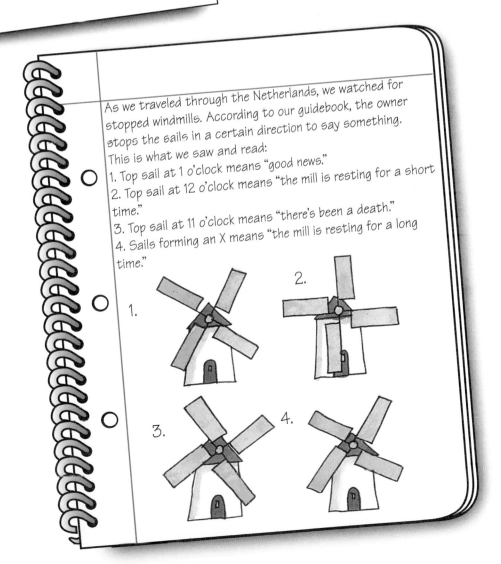

1.

2.

3.

4.

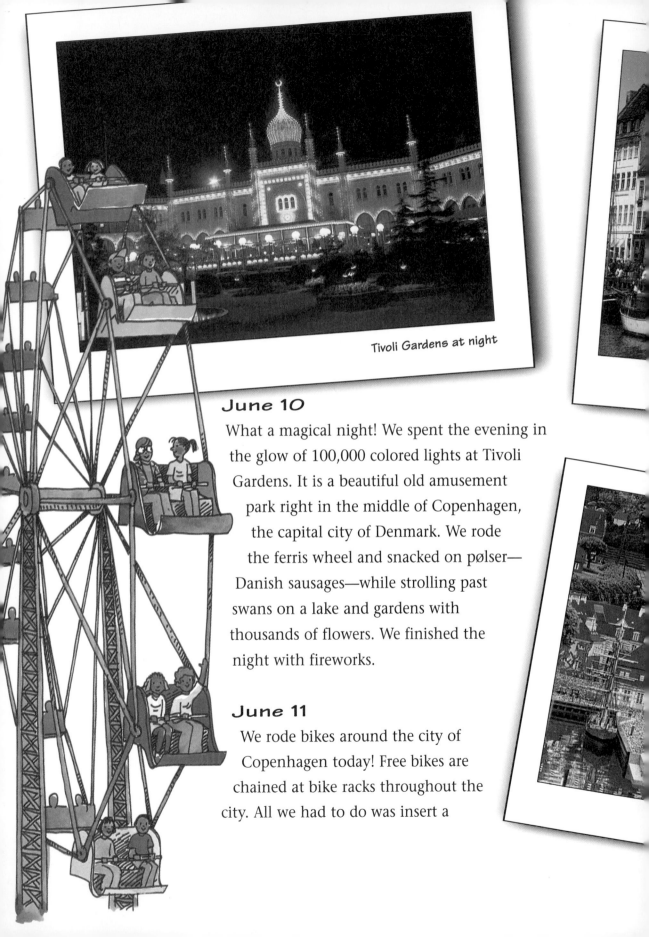

Tivoli Gardens at night

June 10

What a magical night! We spent the evening in the glow of 100,000 colored lights at Tivoli Gardens. It is a beautiful old amusement park right in the middle of Copenhagen, the capital city of Denmark. We rode the ferris wheel and snacked on pølser—Danish sausages—while strolling past swans on a lake and gardens with thousands of flowers. We finished the night with fireworks.

June 11

We rode bikes around the city of Copenhagen today! Free bikes are chained at bike racks throughout the city. All we had to do was insert a

a busy street along Nyhavn Canal, Copenhagen

20-kroner coin and peddle away. Then, at the end of the day, we returned the bike and received the coin back!

June 13

We will never forget the 2,200-year-old Tollund Man we saw today at a museum in Silkeborg. People found him in a bog where he'd been since the Iron Age. His face is so well preserved you can even see the stubble of his beard. He looks so peaceful, but there is still a leather rope around his neck because he was strangled!

June 14

Gabe thought he was the master builder with toy bricks until we saw Legoland in Billund! It is a miniature world right in the middle of Denmark. Everything here is built of toy bricks—over 33 million of them! There are little cities and villages, plus rivers, canals, railroads, airports, and even birds sitting in the trees!

Legoland—a beautiful place to live if you are only inches tall

June 15

We just crossed the North Sea by ferry to Kristiansand, a city on the southern coast of Norway. The sandy beaches here are packed with people on vacation. Farther out, we're told that people fish and drill for oil and gas. The sea is a major trade route connecting the countries that border it—Norway, Denmark, Germany, the Netherlands, Belgium, France, and the United Kingdom—with the rest of the world. We can see how the Vikings long ago sailed this sea to try to conquer and settle new lands.

a Norwegian fiord with steep cliffs and waterfalls

ICELAND

ATLANTIC OCEAN

IRELAND

Dublin ●

June 17

We've been touring Norway's coast and its amazing fiords—long, narrow inlets of the sea. You walk through a thick forest and suddenly there's a steep, rocky drop-off and a crashing, roaring waterfall to the water way below. We camped overnight in the forest.

June 19

Oslo, the capital of Norway, is the place to learn about Vikings. We explored the Vikingskiphuset—a museum devoted to Vikings—and saw Viking burial ships over 1,100 years old! The ships were packed with tools and goods such as pots, tapestries, and ornaments—anything the Vikings thought a dead person might need in the afterlife. Sometimes a servant was packed in there. Yikes!

June 21

We're in Lapland, an area that is partly in far northern Finland, Norway, Sweden, and Russia. It's the home of the reindeer. As we flew into Rovaniemi, we saw the layout of the main streets looks like a reindeer's antlers! At a reindeer farm, we met Sami people, who are also called Lapps. Some of them herd reindeer the way cowboys herd cattle in the United States. The reindeer racing season was over, but we petted some tame reindeer and met a reindeer jockey.

Lapland

Norwegian Sea

Rovaniemi

FINLAND

NORWAY

Oslo

SWEDEN

Helsinki

Stockholm

Kristiansand

Edinburgh

North Sea

DENMARK

Silkeborg

Billund

Copenhagen

Baltic Sea

UNITED KINGDOM

Snowdonia National Park

Hamburg

Elbe River

London

Gravesend

Amsterdam

NETHERLANDS

Berlin

BELGIUM

Rhine River

GERMANY

Seine River

LUXEMBOURG

Paris

FRANCE

SWITZERLAND

AUSTRIA

June 22

Things have been berry good here! Finland is a land of delicious berries. We tasted blueberries, cranberries, lingonberries, and—from Lapland—cloudberries!

Eastern Europe is a region rich in cultures and traditions. It is a land of great natural beauty and many resources. Dramatic developments such as the breakup of the former Soviet Union have left this part of the world in an unsettled state. Still, behind each country's struggle to solve pressing problems are strong people with a proud history.

ATLANTIC
OCEAN

June 24

We arrived in Gdańsk, Poland, by ferry today. We're visiting one of the most important ports in central Europe. Gdańsk sits along the Vistula River, near where it meets the Baltic Sea. It's a perfect location for exporting and importing goods. We saw the huge Gdańsk Crane. It was used for loading heavy cargo in medieval times and later used for putting up masts on ships.

North
Sea

Welcome to Eastern Europe!

Why is the Warsaw ghetto famous?

How many different varieties of roses are there?

What is goulash?

Barents Sea

RUSSIA

Ural Mountains

SWEDEN

FINLAND

St. Petersburg

Volga River

ESTONIA

Moscow

Ural River

LATVIA

Baltic Sea

LITHUANIA

Gdańsk

BELARUS

Frombork

KAZAKHSTAN

Vistula

Warsaw

River

Don River

GERMANY

POLAND

Kraków

Kiev

Volga River

Vltava

Dnepr River

River

Prague

UKRAINE

CZECH REPUBLIC

Caspian Sea

SLOVAKIA

MOLDOVA

AUSTRIA

HUNGARY

Sea of Azov

SLOVENIA

Budapest

Caucasus Mountains

Danube

CROATIA

ROMANIA

River

GEORGIA

BOSNIA-

Black Sea

AZERBAIJAN

HERZEGOVINA

Belgrade

YUGOSLAVIA

BULGARIA

ITALY

Kazanluk

ALBANIA

MACEDONIA

TURKEY

GREECE

Athens

Olympia

Thira Island

Eastern Europe   107

Dear Grandma,
In Frombork, Poland, today, we saw the workplace of one of Yoshi's heroes—Polish astronomer Nicolaus Copernicus. He's considered the father of modern astronomy! On the front of this card, next to Copernicus, is a diagram of his sun-centered theory, which revolutionized astronomy in 1543!

Love,
Julia

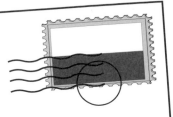

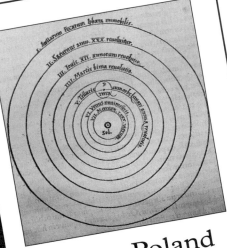

Nicolaus Copernicus—Poland

Kraków has many fine old buildings. The Church of St. Mary and the cloth hall are on the main square.

GUIDEBOOK/POLAND

Looking at Warsaw, Poland's capital city, it's hard to imagine the centuries of fighting that have happened here. Poland has been invaded by neighboring countries time after time. In World War II, Warsaw itself was completely destroyed, but the Poles rebuilt it.

Warsaw's Jewish Ghetto memorial marks a terrible, brave struggle for freedom here. During World War II, Germany conquered Poland. The Nazis, who controlled Poland as well as Germany, confined thousands of Jews to a section of the city called the ghetto. In 1943, the Jews staged a heroic fight for freedom. They were surrounded and poorly armed, but they fought on for nearly a month before they were finally defeated.

June 27

We flew east to Saint Petersburg, Russia, and today we went to the Hermitage, the largest museum in Russia. The largest part of the museum was the Winter Palace for the czars, who once ruled Russia. Yoshi kept talking about the splendid dances the dazzling ballrooms have seen! Outside Saint Petersburg, we visited Peterhof—that's Dutch for "Peter's Court." It is the oldest royal country residence in Russia. There are 10 palaces, huge gardens, and 150 fountains!

June 29

Just standing in Red Square in Moscow was awesome! It is a vast plaza. We immediately recognized the colorful, onion-shaped domes of Saint Basil's Cathedral that we read about in school. And we saw the huge walled fortress called the Kremlin. Inside the Kremlin's high brick walls are palaces and cathedrals built by the czars. Today, the Kremlin is the center of government.

June 30

We rode the Metro to find lunch in Moscow today. The Metro is the subway. Some stations are so beautiful, they look like halls in a palace! We took pictures of them. At lunch, Yoshi liked the borscht (beet soup). Gabe liked stroganoff (beef strips with noodles and sauce). After lunch, we rode paddle boats in Gorki Park. A vendor said we were lucky to be visiting in summer. In winter, much of Russia is very cold, often covered with snow or ice.

one of Moscow's Metro stations—a beautiful place to wait for the subway

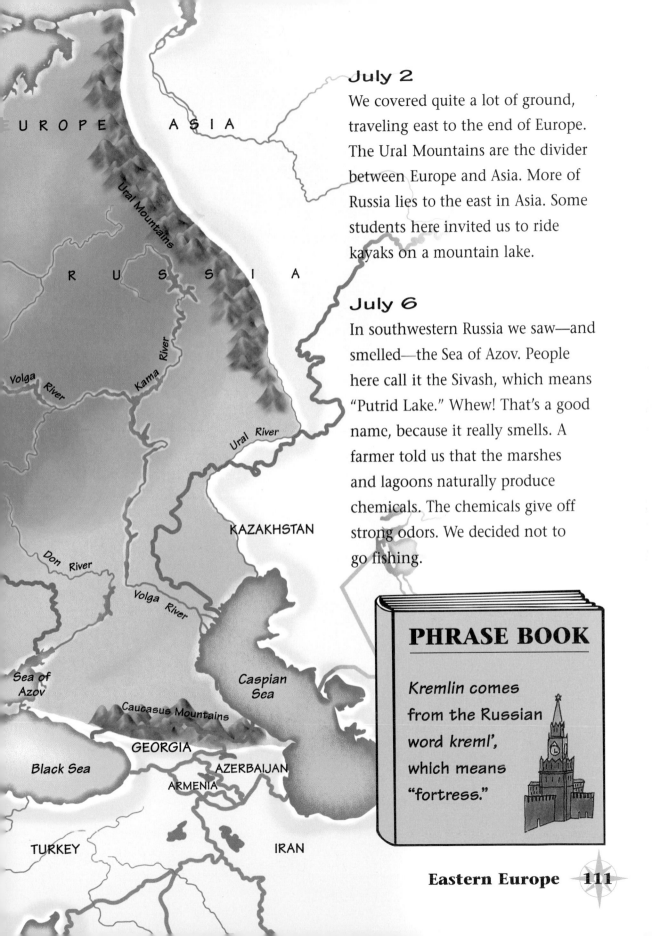

EUROPE

ASIA

Ural Mountains

RUSSIA

Kama River

Volga River

Ural River

KAZAKHSTAN

Don River

Volga River

Sea of Azov

Caspian Sea

Caucasus Mountains

GEORGIA

Black Sea

AZERBAIJAN

ARMENIA

TURKEY

IRAN

July 2

We covered quite a lot of ground, traveling east to the end of Europe. The Ural Mountains are the divider between Europe and Asia. More of Russia lies to the east in Asia. Some students here invited us to ride kayaks on a mountain lake.

July 6

In southwestern Russia we saw—and smelled—the Sea of Azov. People here call it the Sivash, which means "Putrid Lake." Whew! That's a good name, because it really smells. A farmer told us that the marshes and lagoons naturally produce chemicals. The chemicals give off strong odors. We decided not to go fishing.

PHRASE BOOK

Kremlin comes from the Russian word kreml', which means "fortress."

July 10

We visited Prague Castle on a hill not far from the banks of the Vltava River. This once was the home of the kings of Bohemia. It is still used as the office of the president of the Czech Republic. Near Prague Castle, on old winding streets heading down the hill, we walked through lots of other castles, churches, and historic buildings. On Golden Lane (Zlatá ulicka), we passed little tiny houses stuck into the walls and arches along the way. These were where the castle guards once lived. Later, goldsmiths and artists lived there!

Prague Castle at dusk, seen from across the Vltava River

July 13

We like soup and stew, so it is no surprise that we really like goulash. We had a bowl of this famous Hungarian stew today, and it hit the spot! It's made of meat, onions, potatoes, gravy, and—since we're in Hungary—plenty of paprika for seasoning. Paprika is a bright red spice grown in Hungary. It comes from ground-up pods of a kind of pepper plant. But compared to other peppers, it has a taste that is mild and almost sweet. As a bonus, it is one of the richest plant sources of vitamin C. Yum! While we ate, a man played gypsy music on a violin. The cafe owner told us that gypsies have lived in many countries of Europe for hundreds of years, and they are known for their music. Yoshi says the music makes her feel excited—and a little bit sad.

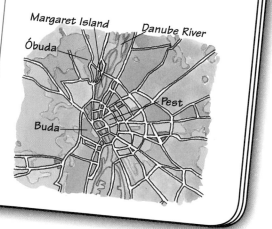

We found out that Budapest, the capital of Hungary, is really three cities and an island. The city is made of the cities of Buda and Óbuda on the west side of the Danube River, Pest on the east side, and Margaret Island in the middle. They all joined together to form the city of Budapest.

Margaret Island
Danube River
Óbuda
Pest
Buda

GUIDEBOOK/BULGARIA

It takes millions of rose petals to make one pound (.45 kilograms) of rose oil. Blossoms are hand picked in the early morning dew, placed in baskets, emptied into sacks, and rushed to the distillery. Flowers can't be used if they are picked later in the day because the hot sun causes precious parts of the oil to evaporate.

There are over 27,000 varieties of roses, but only a few varieties are used to make rose oil. Red or pink Damask roses are considered the best. One kind, the Kazanluk rose, has been grown in Bulgaria's Valley of Roses for more than 150 years.

July 15

Today we went sightseeing—and smelling—in Bulgaria's world-famous Valley of Roses. The valley is dozens of miles long and has a wonderful climate and soil for growing roses. The millions of rose bushes here supply most of the world's most fragrant rose oil. We knew that rose oil—also called attar of roses—is used in perfume. But we did not know that roses are used in medicine and food until we picked up some recipes at a shop.

July 16

Today we each made an old-fashioned Yugoslavian wooden doll. Here's how:

1. Paint or draw a face on the bowl or back of a wooden spoon. (Get permission first!)

2. Glue on fur or yarn for hair.

3. Cut a shirt and pants, or a dress, out of felt or cloth. Make designs on the clothes with sequins or markers. Cover the handle of the spoon with the clothes. Glue the materials to the handle.

4. Fold a square of cloth diagonally to make a head scarf. Fit it around the head. Tie a piece of string around the "neck" to hold the ends tight.

YUGOSLAVIA

Kazanluk

BULGARIA

MACEDONIA

ALBANIA

Tiranë

Thessaloniki

Mount
Olympus

Limnos

Corfu

Larisa

Aegean Sea

Lesbos

G R E E C E

Leucas

Euboea

Chios

Cephalonia

Gulf of Corinth

Patrai

Ionian Sea

Marathon

Athens

Andros

Zante

Olympia

Samos

P e l o p o n n e s u s

Naxos

Thira

Mediterranean Sea

C r e t e

July 17

Gabe won the gold medal in an Olympic race today! Yoshi got the silver. We were in the Olympia valley in Greece, where the first recorded Olympic Games were held, so we had a race of our own. The first winner ever in the Olympics was a runner, too, because running was the only contest at first. After a while, the Greeks added chariot races and other sports. Our guide said that the early Olympic Games were part of a festival they held every four years in honor of their god Zeus.

Nowadays, the Olympic flame that starts each Olympic Games is lit here in Olympia. It's carried from Greece all the way to the site of the games.

Some people believe there once was a continent called Atlantis, which sank into the Atlantic Ocean thousands of years ago. Legends tell that a brilliant civilization once existed there. But the people became corrupt and greedy, and so the gods punished them. One day, great explosions shook Atlantis, and the continent sank into the sea.

Many people have developed theories about where Atlantis was, and some people have tried to find it. Today, many researchers believe Atlantis was actually Thira, home of the Minoan people. Thira was mostly destroyed when a volcano erupted. Part of the volcano collapsed, and the sea flooded it. Most of the people escaped, but their rich culture was destroyed.

July 20

We sailed across the top of an active volcano today! We were visiting Thira in the Aegean Sea. This crescent-shaped island, and several little islands near it, are what remains of a volcano that exploded more than 3,400 years ago. The captain told us it could all explode again anytime! In fact, there are two little "Burnt Isles" that rose up from the water centuries later. These black cones are still smoldering!

July 22

This morning, we ate feta for breakfast. The waiter said that feta is a cheese made from sheep's or goat's milk. After breakfast, we began our tour of Athens. Athens, the capital and largest city of Greece, lies along the Mediterranean Sea.

We started our tour at the top—the top of the main hill, called the Acropolis—and made our way down and around town.

This is the Acropolis in Athens, Greece. The Parthenon, a temple of the goddess Athena, is at the top of the hill.

July 23

We've eaten olives whole and halved, and we've even dipped our bread in olive oil! The Greeks use olive oil a lot in their cooking—and they supply plenty of olive oil to the rest of the world. An olive tree can live to be over 2,000 years old.

a news vendor at his stand in Athens

PHRASE BOOK

The word acropolis comes from the Greek words akro and polis, which mean "high" and "city."

MAP IT!
Europe

North
Sea

UNITED
KINGDOM

NETHERLANDS

Baltic
Sea

ATLANTIC
OCEAN

GERMANY

HUNGARY

Mediterranean Sea

GREECE

Aegean
Sea

We did it. We traveled all the way across another continent—Europe. See the giant thumbtacks on the next page? Inside each one is a picture clue of one of our favorite places in Europe. If the thumbtacks were real, could you pin each one correctly on the map to show in which country the pictured place is? We drew the route to remind you of where our travels took us.

1. jewels to try on

2. a great lunch

3. an old way to tell time

4. sounds good with dinner

5. a look at ancient times

Caspian Sea

Black Sea

Answers:

1. crown jewels, United Kingdom;
2. Edam cheese, Netherlands;
3. glockenspiel, Germany;
4. gypsy music, Hungary;
5. Parthenon, Greece.

Map It! 121

Many people hear names of western Asian countries and think "sand." But rocky plains are just as common in Saudi Arabia as sandy deserts. Plateaus and mountains cover most of Turkey, Azerbaijan, and Yemen. Some of history's best-known rivers flow through the region. For instance, the Jordan River was important in Biblical times. Also, the world's first civilization formed around the Tigris and Euphrates rivers.

July 24

A bus took us from Athens to the Turkish city of Istanbul. The tour guide said it's a place where Europe meets Asia. So part of Turkey must be in Europe and the other part in Asia.

Welcome to Western Asia!

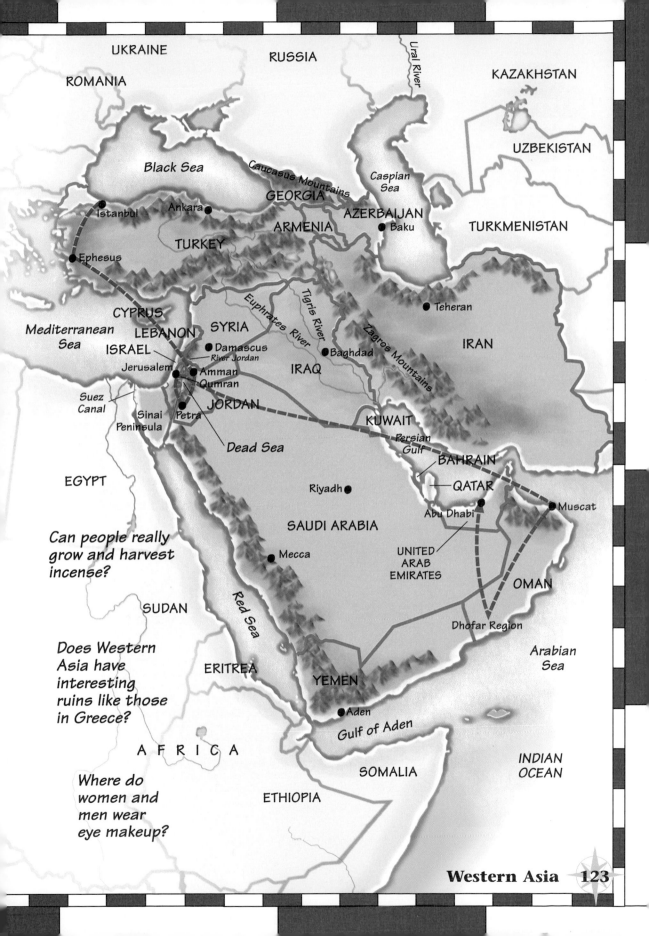

UKRAINE

ROMANIA

RUSSIA

Ural River

KAZAKHSTAN

Black Sea

Caucasus Mountains

GEORGIA

Caspian Sea

UZBEKISTAN

Istanbul

Ankara

AZERBAIJAN

ARMENIA

Baku

TURKMENISTAN

Ephesus

TURKEY

CYPRUS

Teheran

Euphrates River

Tigris River

Zagros Mountains

IRAN

Mediterranean Sea

LEBANON

SYRIA

Damascus

ISRAEL

River Jordan

Baghdad

Jerusalem

Amman

IRAQ

Qumran

Suez Canal

JORDAN

Petra

KUWAIT

Sinai Peninsula

Persian Gulf

Dead Sea

BAHRAIN

EGYPT

QATAR

Riyadh

Muscat

Abu Dhabi

Can people really grow and harvest incense?

SAUDI ARABIA

UNITED ARAB EMIRATES

Mecca

OMAN

Red Sea

Dhofar Region

Does Western Asia have interesting ruins like those in Greece?

SUDAN

Arabian Sea

ERITREA

YEMEN

Aden

Gulf of Aden

INDIAN OCEAN

A F R I C A

Where do women and men wear eye makeup?

SOMALIA

ETHIOPIA

July 25

The guide also told us that 99 percent of the people in Turkey are Muslims. So naturally Istanbul's most historic holy place was once a mosque, or Islamic place of worship. But according to the guide-book, the mosque started out as the church of Hagia Sophia, or "Holy Wisdom." The Roman Emperor Justinian had it built about 1,500 years ago. It has marble walls and a domed ceiling decorated with mosaics—pictures made of tile pieces.

GUIDEBOOK/TURKEY

After the Muslims took control of the city, Hagia Sophia was made into a mosque. The mosaics were covered because Islam teaching forbids pictures and statues of living things. Outside the mosque, minarets (prayer towers), were added. You can see them in the photo above. In 1935, the Turks turned the mosque into a museum and uncovered the mosaics for all to marvel.

July 26

Istanbul in July is hot, hot, hot. What a relief to cool off underground while visiting the Sunken Palace! Actually, this huge structure was never a palace. The brochure we picked up at the hotel says that it was built as a cistern, an underground room used to store water. For hundreds of years, the people of Istanbul drew water from the Sunken Palace when the city was under attack or when wells went dry in the summer heat. What a storeroom!

This underground palace in Istanbul was really a cistern—a place to store water.

July 27

From Istanbul, we took a plane and a bus to Ephesus. Meanwhile, Yoshi read aloud about how, long ago, Ephesus was a Greek colony and then a Roman colony. Visitors came by sea because Ephesus was a major port of the ancient world. For centuries, the Cayster River deposited silt, or fine soil, in the harbor. Over time, this soil formed a 3-mile stretch of flat land between Ephesus and the sea, and the river disappeared.

Ruins are about all that remain. But judging by the foundations and broken pillars, the buildings must have been huge. According to Yoshi, visitors from all over came to worship at the Temple of Artemis, a Greek goddess. Julia claims that in Greek myths, Artemis kept lions, deer, and other wild animals healthy so hunters would always have plenty of game.

July 29

We flew to Queen Alia Airport in Jordan just in time to catch a tour bus. After miles of treeless, mountainous landscape, we passed through a narrow pass called the Siq (seek). At the end was an awesome building cut into the side of a cliff. The tour guide said the Nabataeans probably used it as a royal tomb. The Nabataeans came to the canyon in the late 400's B.C. and carved Petra, an entire city, out of the red sandstone there. They also built channels and cisterns that collected and stored rainwater. For more than 500 years, the Nabataeans charged tolls from camel caravans passing through with precious oils and silks.

Next stop: Jerusalem.

PHRASE BOOK

Petra comes from the Greek word for "rock."

In Jordan, we saw this entrance gate to Petra. Petra was an entire city that was carved out of the stone mountainside!

July 30

We spent the day in the Old City, or walled part of Jerusalem. According to signs, the Temple Mount is where the Jews' Father Abraham almost sacrificed his son Isaac. Muslims also believe that their prophet Muhammad rose to heaven from that spot. They built a shrine there called the Dome of the Rock. We visited the shrine and then walked to the Church of the Holy Sepulchre. Christians built the church to mark where Jesus was crucified and buried.

A street vendor sold us some felafel, which were crisp, deep-fried patties of mashed chickpeas. We gobbled them down, left the Old City, and hopped a bus for the Dead Sea.

August 1

We visited caves in Qumran, Israel, where a group of Jews called the Essenes wrote the Dead Sea Scrolls. The scrolls are the oldest copies of writings from the Bible.

The Dead Sea is so salty that not even fish can live in it. But the owner of a health resort claimed that the minerals in the water are good for people. They calm the nerves and soothe the skin.

caves in Qumran, Israel

We saw this baby tahr and its mom in Oman.

August 3

Yesterday our plane landed northwest of Muscat, Oman's capital. We headed straight to the outdoor market. Yoshi bought a silver box that was decorated with old coins. Inside was a black powder called kohl. The shopkeeper told us that women and men use kohl to make up their eyes.

Steven decided to buy a turban like the ones all the Omani men were wearing.

From the market we headed west to Qurm Public Park and National Reserve. We saw a baby Arabian tahr and its mother. They looked kind of like goats. Supposedly when a tahr senses danger, it whistles to alert its companions, and they all run for the hills.

August 3

Dear Dad,
We are in an area called Dhofar in southern Oman. I bet you'll never guess what gets harvested from these trees. It's frankincense. Dhofar is one of the few places the trees will grow. We watched as workers cut into the bark of the tree trunks and harvested the fragrant frankincense gum. It is used in making medicine and for burning as incense. Our guidebook says that in Biblical times, frankincense was among the world's most precious substances.

Love,
Julia

Oman

Women in the United Arab Emirates wear abayahs. Some women keep their faces covered.

August 5

Our next stop was in the United Arab Emirates. These are seven small states that joined under one government. The richest state is called Abu Dhabi. Its largest city, which is the nation's capital, is also Abu Dhabi. We visited the Handicrafts Center. Some women worked with *al khoo*s, a palm tree frond that they braided into mats and baskets. Other women made jugs and incense burners from clay. Some women wove sheep wool and goat hair into carpets, blankets, and tents.

The women wore black robes called *abayahs*. Most women covered their hair with black scarves, and some covered their faces.

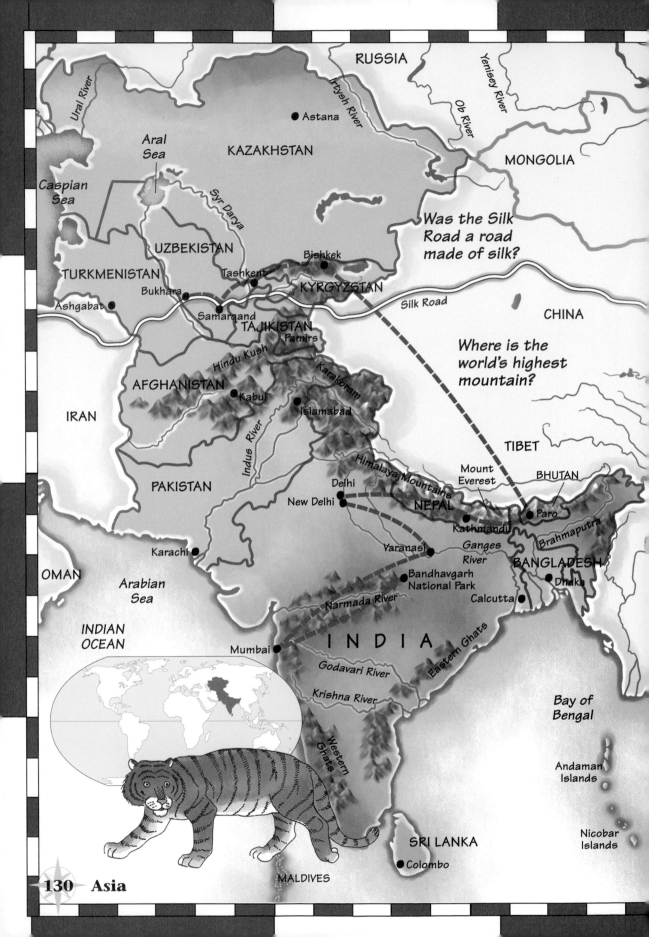

RUSSIA

Yenisey River

Ob River

Irtysh River

• Astana

Ural River

KAZAKHSTAN

MONGOLIA

Aral
Sea

Caspian
Sea

Syr Darya

**Was the Silk
Road a road
made of silk?**

UZBEKISTAN

• Bishkek

Tashkent

CHINA

TURKMENISTAN

Bukhara

KYRGYZSTAN

Silk Road

Ashgabat •

• Samarqand

TAJIKISTAN

Pamirs

**Where is the
world's highest
mountain?**

Hindu Kush

Karakoram

AFGHANISTAN

• Kabul

IRAN

Islamabad •

Indus River

TIBET

BHUTAN

Mount
Everest

PAKISTAN

Himalaya Mountains

Delhi •

New Delhi •

NEPAL

• Paro

Brahmaputra

Karachi •

Kathmandu
•

Varanasi •

Ganges
River

BANGLADESH

OMAN

Arabian
Sea

Bandhavgarh
National Park

• Dhaka

Calcutta
•

Narmada River

INDIAN
OCEAN

I N D I A

Eastern Ghats

Mumbai •

Godavari River

Bay of
Bengal

Krishna River

Western
Ghats

Andaman
Islands

SRI LANKA

Nicobar
Islands

• Colombo

MALDIVES

Welcome to Central and Southern Asia!

Central and southern Asia is rich in people and history. The region includes the Himalayan countries—India, Nepal, Bhutan, Pakistan, Afghanistan, and Tibet—and Bangladesh and Sri Lanka. It also includes some republics that were once part of the Soviet Union. They are now the independent nations of Kazakhstan, Tajikistan, Kyrgyzstan, Uzbekistan, and Turkmenistan.

August 6

We flew to Bukhara in Uzbekistan and boarded a train for Samarqand, another ancient Uzbekistan city. Bukhara and Samarqand were stops on the legendary Silk Road. Camel caravans used it to carry silks and spices from the Far East to ports in west Asia, where European ships came to trade.

Why are tigers disappearing?

Is a dopy worn on the head, the hand, or the foot?

Look at the Registan's tiles!

August 7

Our favorite sight in Samarqand was the Registan, a mosque built around 1400 by Timur. He was the Mongol warrior who ruled what is now Uzbekistan. The entire outside of the mosque is decorated with a colorful tilework called majolica.

August 8

From Samarqand, we rode the train to Tashkent. As we rode, we didn't see any plants or animals on the land. Yoshi read that the former Soviet Union's farming policies drained the soil of nutrients that plants and wildlife need.

A huge earthquake in 1966 destroyed most of early Tashkent. Most buildings now are concrete apartment houses. However, the Chorsu

The Chorsu Bazaar in Tashkent served up lots of yummy food!

Bazaar, a huge open market, gave us a taste of life in the old city. Uzbek men were dressed in dark coats and dopys, or four-sided skullcaps, and the women wore glittery pants and knee-length tunics.

August 9

Our next step was the capital of Kyrgyzstan. A fairly new city founded in 1825, Bishkek was named after the churn that nomads use to make fermented mare's milk. Most of the country is mountainous, and the snowy slopes were too inviting. We went "sledding" on our plastic trash bags!

This is how big the sea used to be.

The sea has shrunk to this size.

Uzbekistan has long been a cotton-growing center. The Soviet Union took over the area (then part of an area called Turkestan) in the early 1900's. In the 1960's, the Soviet Union decided that Uzbekistan's farmers should grow even more cotton. So the farmers developed larger cotton fields through irrigation, a system that carries river water to dry land. This water came from rivers that flow into the Aral Sea. Today Uzbekistan is an independent nation, but it still uses river water for irrigation. The Aral Sea is now only one-half the size it was in 1960.

August 10

Today we flew to Paro in Bhutan. We trekked Bhutan's cold northern forests, looking for red pandas, blue sheep, and other animals that no longer live in other Himalayan countries. We wanted to scout the southern jungles for pygmy hogs and one-horned rhinoceroses, but our guidebook said that it was a conservation area. It was closed to visitors to protect its wildlife. Many of Bhutan's conservation laws are rooted in Buddhist beliefs.

A red panda has long, reddish-brown fur and a long, bushy tail.

August 11

This morning we landed in central Nepal's Kathmandu Valley. To the south we could see the Mahabharat Mountains. These reach heights up to 9,000 feet. But they look like hills compared to the Himalaya Range. Eight of the world's ten highest mountains, including the highest, Mount Everest, are in the Himalaya of northern Nepal.

In Kathmandu, Nepal's capital, Hindus were celebrating the festival of Naag Panchami. According to legend, snakes, especially cobras, can bring wealth or disaster. So to win the snakes' favor, people visit shrines and offer milk and flowers to live cobras or their images. Outside one shrine, we watched a snake charmer playing a pipe and his trained cobra swaying.

August 12

Today we arrived in New Delhi, India's capital. It was built just south of Delhi, India's second largest city, about 70 years ago. We visited the Parliament House, a big, round building, and rode around the city to look at some beautiful homes and gardens.

Our guide said that movies are very popular in India and that Indian movie studios make hundreds of new films each year. He named some of the most popular films, and we went to see one. Even though the story was serious, the movie was filled with beautiful singing and dancing.

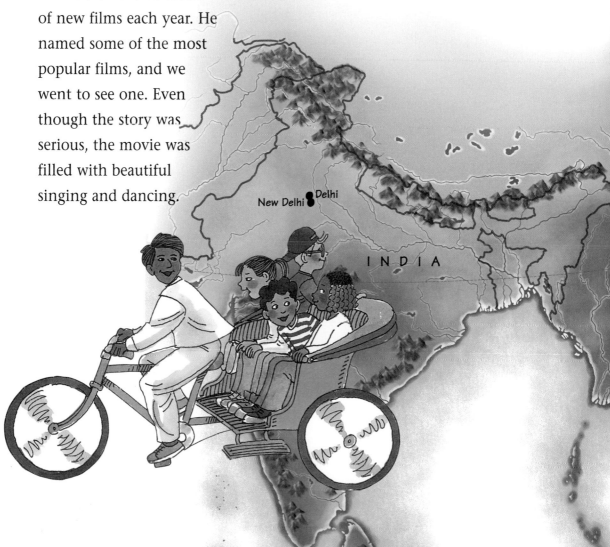

New Delhi Delhi

I N D I A

August 16

Dear Molly,
Talking about tigers and danger made us think of the Indian boy Mowgli in Rudyard Kipling's *The Jungle Book*. A tiger tried to kill him. Now the tables are turned, and tigers are in danger.

Bye,
Julia

THE JUNGLE BOOK

August 13

We met several Hindus on their way to the city of Varanasi. They were going there to bathe in the Ganges, India's most holy river. Some people bathe to clean their spirits. Others hope the holy waters will cure their illnesses. We also saw people using the river to wash themselves and do laundry.

The water sure looked dirty. According to the guidebook, concerned people called environmentalists developed the Ganges Plan in the 1980's. The plan included releasing turtles into the river to eat up decaying garbage. Poachers, or outlaw hunters, killed most of the turtles for meat. But environmentalists are still trying to find ways to clean the Ganges.

Ganesh, an elephant-headed god, is one of many forms of gods and goddesses worshiped in the Hindu religion.

August 14

In the city of Mumbai, Hindus were celebrating the festival of Ganesh Chaturthi. People were parading through the streets and stopping traffic. Many people were dancing and singing, and some were carrying a huge plaster statue of the god Ganesh. We followed them to Chowpatty Beach, where they plunged the statue of Ganesh into the Arabian Sea. Young girls came up to us and draped ropes of flowers around our necks. All day and night, fireworks were exploding in the sky.

August 16

We mounted elephants and followed a guide through the grasslands and forests of Bandhavgarh National Park. A herd of spotted deer called chital sped away as we approached. Nearby we spied a tigress toting her cub by the skin on the back of its neck.

The guide explained that poachers kill dozens of India's tigers each year. They sell the tigers' bones to companies who add them to traditional Chinese medicines. An even greater danger to tigers is the decrease in chital and other prey that tigers need to survive.

Japan is the most modern nation in Asia. In much of Mongolia, people's lives have changed much more slowly. Tourists have been visiting Hong Kong and Macao for hundreds of years. But few outsiders travel to Siberia or North Korea. Eastern Asia is a study in opposites.

What are sashimi, tofu, fugu, and sumo?

Welcome to Eastern Asia!

August 19

We took an early flight to Ürümqi. According to the guidebook, it's the capital of Xinjiang, a northwestern province of China. The weather here is sizzling, but someone on the plane said that to the southeast, in Turpan, the temperature once reached a record 121.3 °F. And supposedly the winters are far below freezing. No wonder fewer people live here than in eastern China!

EUROPE

Ural Mountains

INDIA

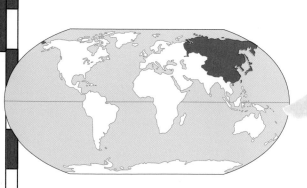

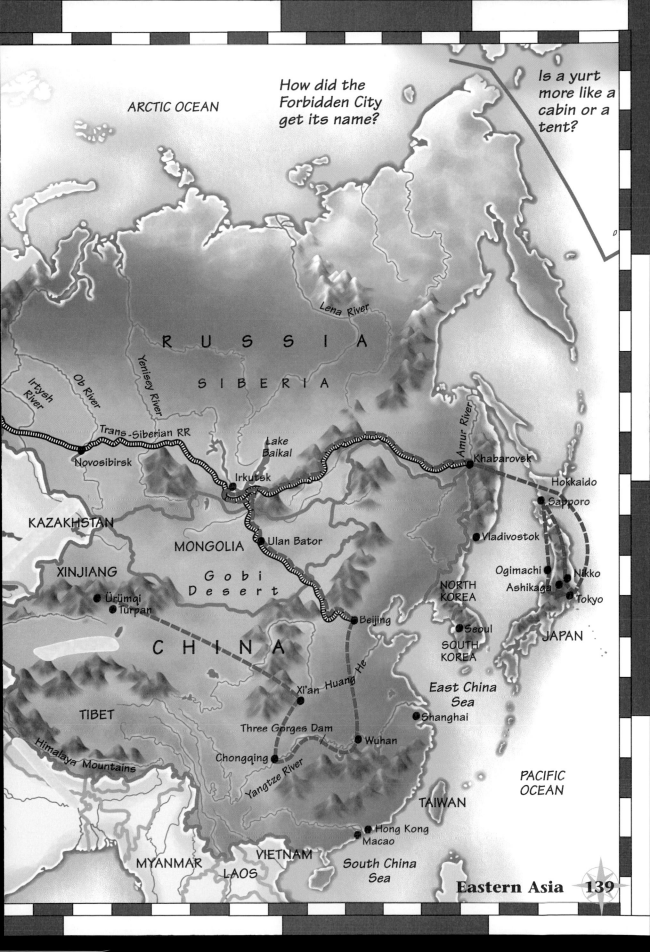

ARCTIC OCEAN

How did the
Forbidden City
get its name?

Is a yurt
more like a
cabin or a
tent?

Lena River

R U S S I A

S I B E R I A

Irtysh
River

Ob River

Yenisey River

Amur River

Trans-Siberian RR

Novosibirsk

Lake
Baikal

Irkutsk

Khabarovsk

Hokkaido

Sapporo

KAZAKHSTAN

MONGOLIA

Ulan Bator

Vladivostok

XINJIANG

G o b i
D e s e r t

Ogimachi

Nikko

Ürümqi

Ashikaga

Turpan

Tokyo

C H I N A

Beijing

NORTH
KOREA

Seoul

JAPAN

SOUTH
KOREA

East China
Sea

Xi'an

Huang He

TIBET

Shanghai

Three Gorges Dam

Wuhan

Himalaya
Mountains

Chongqing

Yangtze River

TAIWAN

PACIFIC
OCEAN

Hong Kong

Macao

MYANMAR

VIETNAM

South China
Sea

LAOS

August 20

At 8 this morning, we caught a bus and rode halfway up a mountain to Tianchi, or "Lake of Heaven." We leased some Mongolian ponies and rode all the way up to the snow line—the edge of the year-round snow at the mountaintop.

Steve, the horse nut, says the ponies are 12 to 14 hands from the ground to the back above their shoulders. (A hand is about 4 inches.) Their breed was developed by Central Asian nomads as they moved from place to place with their herds of animals. They were the first people to tame wild horses and to use them for pulling carts and carrying packs.

We've decided to spend the night here in a yurt—a round felt tent supported by a wood frame. Like the nomads who live in yurts, we'll sleep on red mats spread on the floor. After that 10-hour ride, those mats look like featherbeds.

We slept in a yurt in China. A yurt can easily be taken down and set up someplace else.

Young Chinese Painter Shows Style

Wang Yani has been painting since the age of 2. This is a painting she did when she was 10. Now a teen-ager, she has created more than ten thousand pictures and shown them on three continents. Today Yani uses the *xieyi hua*, or free style, method of traditional Chinese painting.

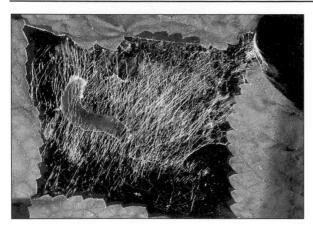

Silk worms feed on mulberry leaves until they are 70 times their original size. Then each worm spews out a fluid that hardens into a thread when it hits the air. The thread winds round the worm and forms a casing called a cocoon. The single thread that makes up a cocoon sometimes measures 3/4 mile long.

The farmer allows some worms to remain in their cocoons and develop into moths. The other cocoons are heated to kill the developing insects inside. Then the farmer unwinds the cocoons to harvest the thread.

August 24

This morning we flew from Ürümqui to China's ancient capital of Xi'an. Here, according to legend, a Chinese empress discovered the secret of making silk. To see the secret for ourselves, we visited a nearby silkworm farm.

Earlier in the summer, the farmer had collected hundreds of tiny eggs laid by moths called Bombyx mori.

Now the eggs are in cold storage. Next spring, they will hatch into silkworms.

When we returned to the city, we visited a silk shop. Yoshi and Julia bought silk to take home.

August 29

We are seeing so much in China—yet there is so much more to see! From Xi'an we flew to Chongqing on the Yangtze, the world's third longest river. We spent the night aboard the

Regal China cruise ship and started up the river in the morning.

The most awesome sights on the cruise were the Three Gorges, where cliffs rise up on either side of the river. There we watched workers busy building the world's largest dam. It will create a giant reservoir, or human-made lake. That means water will fill the gorges and cover the plains along the river. The dam will keep the river from flooding, but all this cool scenery will be gone. Worse yet, thousands of farmers will lose their land.

Can you see the cliffs of the Yangtze in the background?

Three Gorges Dam

Wuhan

Chongqing

Yangtze River

Dongting Lake

Poyang Lake

C H I N A

The Forbidden City got that name because for 500 years no uninvited visitors could enter. Only the royal families and members of their households were allowed.

August 31

From Wuhan, we flew to Beijing, the capital of China. In the heart of Beijing lies a city within the city. It contains the palaces of Chinese emperors, and it's called the Forbidden City.

To reach the Forbidden City, we crossed a moat, or trench filled with water, and entered a gate in a 35-foot wall. Inside the wall were six palaces and dozens of other buildings with a total of 9,000 rooms.

September 1

From Beijing we took the Trans-Mongolian Railway to Ulan Bator, the capital of Mongolia. Once there, we hitched a ride in a jeep to a tourist camp northeast of the city. On the way, we counted hundreds of grazing horses, yaks, and sheep. The guidebook says that Mongolia has ten times more livestock than people, and now we believe it! The other campers greeted us with shorlog, or barbecued mutton on a skewer.

September 3

We continued on the Trans-Mongolian Railway to Irkutsk in Russia. There we caught the Trans-Siberian Railway going east. From his window, Gabe spotted Lake Baikal, which is the deepest lake in the world. The guidebook says it holds one-fifth of the earth's unfrozen fresh water and more kinds of water life than any other lake. Yoshi insisted the only thing she could see was the smoke from the surrounding factories.

September 6

Our train ride ended in the Siberian city of Khabarovsk—just in time to catch an airliner headed for Tokyo, the capital of Japan.

In Tokyo, we found a traditional Japanese inn called a ryokan. At the entrance, we left our shoes in a rack and put on slippers that the innkeeper gave us. A maid took us to our rooms and motioned for us to remove our slippers.

The floors inside are covered with thick mats that the maid called tatami. They are made of straw, and Julia says they smell like the hayloft back home. Right now, the maid is pulling quilts, pillows, and futons, or mattresses, from the closet. Steven is complaining that the pillows feel hard. That's because they're filled with rice husks instead of feathers. We've read that rice-husk pillows keep your head cool, and in Japan a cool head is considered a sign of good health.

Tokyo's Ashibé Restaurant

Tofu: bean curd. Order it chilled or deep fried.

◆◆

Miso shiru: soup made of soybean paste

◆◆

Udon: fat white noodles made from wheat

◆◆

Sashimi: pieces of plain raw fish served with a fiery-flavored soy sauce dip

◆◆

Fugu: also called blowfish, prepared by government-licensed chefs who remove all the deadly poison before serving

September 7

This morning a tour bus took us north of Tokyo and dropped us in Nikko National Park. At the visitor center, we bought our tickets to cross the pretty Shinkyo Bridge. Julia said it was worth the 300 yen to imagine herself walking there in a traditional silk kimono and special white makeup.

Nikko's chief attraction, Toshogu Shrine, is actually the 380-year-old tomb of a Japanese shogun, or war lord. Toshogu has lots of colorful carvings. The guide said it was in the Korean style and offended very traditional Japanese, who prefer simple shrines with very little decoration.

We visited a distant cousin of Yoshi in his two-story house built of posts and beams. All of a sudden the floor shook, and we hit the tatamis. Yoshi's cousin laughed. We had just experienced a real—though minor—earthquake! But luckily, we were in his house. Like many buildings in Japan, his house was specially built to sway but not fall!

September 8

We wanted to visit the northern island of Hokkaido. So we went to the Tokyo train station and grabbed a train for our 16-hour trip to Hokkaido's capital of Sapporo.

We stayed in Sapporo long enough to visit the Museum of Winter Sports. Sapporo hosted the 1972 Winter Olympics and has one of the longest ski jumps in Japan. Then we hopped another train to the city of Asahigawa to visit nearby Daisetsuzan National Park.

Hokkaido is now the home of the Ainu, who were the original people of Japan. They lived on northern Honshu until the 700's and survived by hunting and fishing. The more powerful Yamato Japanese forced them north. Today most Ainu have blended with the rest of Japanese society, and only a few live in separate communities.

We were hoping to spot a Hokkaido brown bear. This is the time of year that brown bears get ready for winter hibernation by bulking up on rich foods. So maybe it's lucky that we didn't meet any. We did see migrating swans from Siberia on their way to the island's east coast.

September 9

Once back in Asahigawa, we found the entire city decorated with flowers. The people were celebrating Kiku no Sekku, or the Chrysanthemum Festival. In Japan, the guidebook says, chrysanthemums stand for all kinds of things: autumn, harvest, wealth, long life, and more.

a busy street crossing in Tokyo

September 10

We took a bus back to Tokyo, so we could stop in the village of Ogimachi. A villager told us that the houses are called gassho-zukuri, which means "hands folded in prayer." That's what the steep roofs look like. They are made of strawlike thatch, just as roofs there have been made for hundreds of years.

We made it to Tokyo in time to watch a sumo match. Sumo is the Japanese form of wrestling. The opponents paired off and stamped around the ring. Then they charged at each other. The wrestler that pushed or threw his opponent out of the ring was the winner. The matches were short, but there were many bouts. We saw the wrestlers use dozens of holds and throws.

Sumo wrestling is one popular sport in Japan.

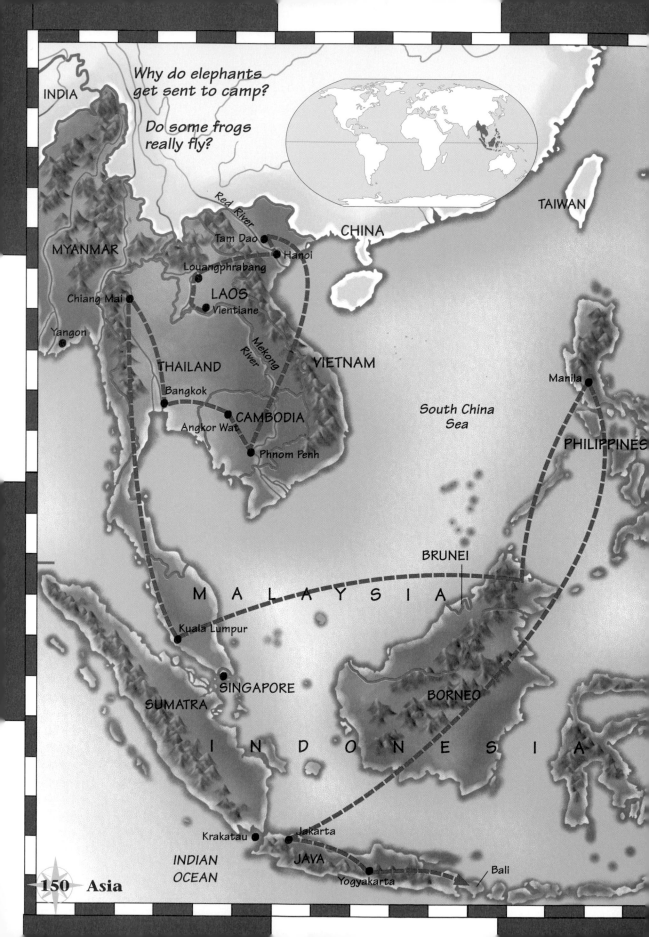

Why do elephants get sent to camp?

Do some frogs really fly?

INDIA

MYANMAR

Yangon

Chiang Mai

THAILAND

Bangkok

Angkor Wat

Red River

Tam Dao

Hanoi

Louangphrabang

LAOS

Vientiane

Mekong River

VIETNAM

CHINA

TAIWAN

CAMBODIA

Phnom Penh

South China Sea

Manila

PHILIPPINES

BRUNEI

MALAYSIA

Kuala Lumpur

SINGAPORE

SUMATRA

BORNEO

INDONESIA

Krakatau

Jakarta

JAVA

Yogyakarta

Bali

INDIAN OCEAN

Why aren't there any trumpets in a gamelan orchestra?

Does a jeepney fly, roll, or float?

PACIFIC OCEAN

Southeast Asia is located north of Australia, south of China, and east of India. Many Westerners have heard the region's exotic-sounding place names—Bangkok, Bali, and Java, to name a few. But few Westerners know about the land and people of Southeast Asia's countries.

September 12

We arrived in the airport at Laos's capital, Vientiane, in the middle of a downpour. The city lies on the Mekong River. The captain told us that the Mekong flows the entire length of the country. It is the major highway, especially during the rainy season—right now. We didn't have to leave the airport, because we caught a flight north to Louangphrabang.

Welcome to Southeast Asia!

September 14

The cliffs and mountains we saw from our windows took our breath away. We wondered how Laotians could make a living on such rugged land. Then everything turned to green, and we realized we were flying over rice paddies.

A Laotian on the plane was eating catfish and ground peanuts rolled up in lettuce leaves. He told Steven this was a popular dish in his country. He also had lots of sticky rice. Some of it he molded into scoops. He used them to eat like we would use spoons.

Once in Louangphrabang, we boarded a boat for a short ride up the Mekong to visit the Pak Ou caves. The ancient caves are considered sacred by Buddhists, and they contain images of Buddha. Julia's favorite was the Buddha "Calling for Rain." He holds his hands pointed down and palms turned in.

statues in one of the Pak Ou caves

We could have looked at the carvings of giant stone faces in this Cambodian Temple for hours!

September 15

We flew to Hanoi, Vietnam's capital. At the airport, Gabe persuaded a jeep driver to take us to Tam Dao National Park. There we met a group of herpetologists, or reptile experts. They invited us to help search for a 14-foot cobra. One herpetologist told Steve that Tam Dao has 108 species of snakes. We never found the cobra. But we did see a ratlike brush-tailed porcupine and a gliding frog, which spread its webbed feet and flew down from the trees.

September 16

Next we flew south to Cambodia's capital, Phnom Penh. Our ride from the airport was a bumpy one. There are potholes in streets and piles of rubble where buildings once stood. The bus driver told us that Phnom Penh was a war zone 20 years ago, when a group called the Khmer Rouge terrorized the country. He said that roads in much of the country were destroyed or damaged.

We took a boat up the Tonle Sap River to Angkor Wat. The guidebook calls it a collection of Hindu wats, or temples, between 800 and 1,200 years old. To get to the temples, we crossed a long bridge over a moat. We found hundreds of sculptures, 200-foot-high towers, and stone walls carved with pictures that told stories about Hindu gods.

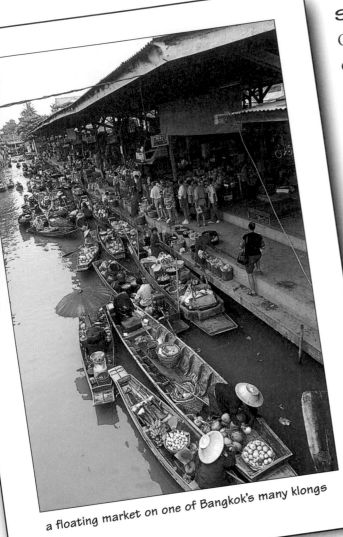
a floating market on one of Bangkok's many klongs

September 18

Our next stop was Thailand's capital, Bangkok. We checked in at a hotel called the Grand Hyatt Erawan. We wondered why people were burning incense and placing flowers before images of a three-headed elephant at the hotel. The desk clerk told us that when the hotel was being built, workers died mysteriously and the marble for the lobby was lost at sea. Hindu spirit doctors persuaded the builders to set up a shrine to the god Brahma and his three-headed elephant, Erawan. Once they did, their problems ended and the hotel was completed.

From the hotel, we walked to one of the city's klongs, or canals, and took a river taxi to the Royal Barge Museum. The boats on display there looked like creatures from Hindu myths. Gabe spent 20 minutes admiring the royal flag barge, which is shaped like a swan. That barge is used by Thailand's king on special occasions.

September 20

From Bangkok, we flew north to Chiang Mai. The cool, dry weather was ideal for trekking. So we had a jeep drop us off along the highway. From there we hiked into the mountains.

After hours of walking, we reached the village of one of Thailand's many hill tribes. According to the guidebook, these are groups that came from China about 100 years ago. They make their living burning trees in the Thai forests and planting crops in the ashes.

The villagers we met were Hmong. Yoshi was curious about the women's hairdos. So a Hmong girl untied the large bun on her head to show us that it was all her own. She said she would never cut her hair because long hair is good luck.

Hmong women let their hair grow long and tie it up in a bun. To them, long hair is good luck.

Thailand

September 23

Dear Dad,

Today we took a bus trip from Chiang Mai to Thailand's official elephant training camp. Mahouts, or elephant keepers, had their trainees show us how they pull heavy logs. That's what elephants did when they worked in Thailand's lumber industry. According to one mahout, Asians have trained elephants for thousands of years. The animals are strong and smart, and they travel well during the rainy season. Their feet become smaller when lifted, so they slip easily out of deep mud.

Love,
Steven

September 24

This morning we arrived at the airport outside of Kuala Lumpur, Malaysia's capital. On the bus ride into the city, Julia read about how Kuala Lumpur has communities of Muslims, Buddhists, and Hindus. We saw people racing across pits filled with hot coals at the Sri Mariamman—the city's oldest Hindu temple. A passerby explained that the city's Indian people were celebrating the Firewalking Festival. The festival honors Sita and other Hindu goddessess who have the power to walk through fire.

September 28

From Kuala Lumpur, we flew to the Malaysian part of the island of Borneo. The rain forests of Borneo and Sumatra, another island, are home to wild orangutans. At the Sepilok Orangutan Rehabilitation Center, we met rangers stocking a platform with food. We hid and waited. Sure enough, half a dozen orangutans arrived to chow down on milk and bananas. A ranger told us that these orangutans had been rescued from logging camps or from being kept illegally as pets. The center helps them return to the wild.

an orangutan mother and baby

September 30

This morning we flew to Manila, the capital of the Philippines. Manila and its suburbs are huge! We wanted to see some of the beautiful countryside, with its rice fields, and visit some fishing villages. Our guide hired a small bus called a jeepney for the trip. He said that some people call jeepneys "folk art on wheels." When ours arrived, we could see why.

farmers planting rice in the Philippines

October 1

Our first stop in Indonesia was the capital, Jakarta. We arrived at the National Museum just in time to see a gamelan, or Indonesian orchestra, perform. Most of the instruments belonged to what our music teacher calls the percussion family. Some of them looked like xylophones made of wood or bronze. There were also bronze gongs. When the player hit one with a thick stick, the boom made Gabe jump in his seat.

Next we visited Indonesia's cultural center, Yogyakarta. There we watched a kind of puppet play called *wayang kulit*. The audience does not see the actual puppets during the play, only their

A gamelan is an Indonesian orchestra.

shadows. We went backstage to meet the cast. The puppets look like paper dolls on sticks and are made from the skins of goats or water buffalo.

Later we watched a puppetmaker who was preparing a new character for the play. He placed a pattern for the head and body of the puppet on a hide that looked like a sheet of paper. Next, he scratched an outline around the pattern and cut separate pieces for the arms. Then he used pointed metal awls and a wooden mallet to punch holes that made up the

A gamelan played as we watched puppets in Indonesia.

features of the puppet's face and the details of its clothing. He fastened a bamboo handle to the puppet's body. He used metal studs to attach the arms so that the shoulders could shrug and the elbows bend. Last, he fastened sticks to the arms. The dalang, or puppet master, would use the sticks as controls to make the puppet come alive.

October 2

Our last stop in Indonesia was the island of Bali. A street vendor sold us tickets to a topeng, or masked drama, at the Tourist Center in the village of Ubud. The drama was actually a story in dance accompanied by a gamelan. The story was about the struggle between a witch and a dragon. We could tell who was who by the masks the actors wore. After the performance, Steve got a close look at one of the actor's masks. It was carved from wood, and the eyes were made from bits of a mirror. On the back of the mask was a crossbar that the actor grips with his teeth to hold the mask in place.

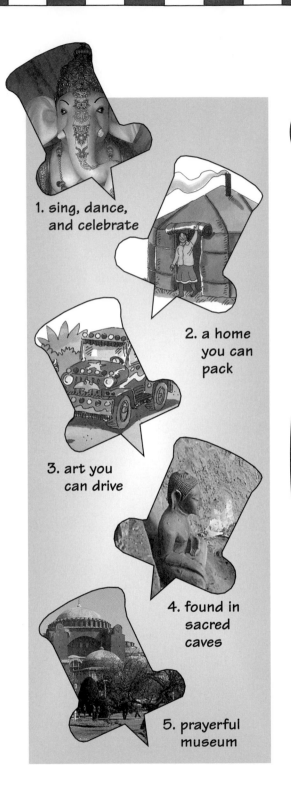

1. sing, dance, and celebrate

2. a home you can pack

3. art you can drive

4. found in sacred caves

5. prayerful museum

MAP IT! Asia

We did it. We traveled all the way across the largest continent—Asia. See the giant thumbtacks on this page? Inside each one is a picture clue of one of our favorite places in Asia. If the thumbtacks were real, could you pin each one correctly on the map to show in which country the pictured place is? We drew the route to remind you of where our travels took us.

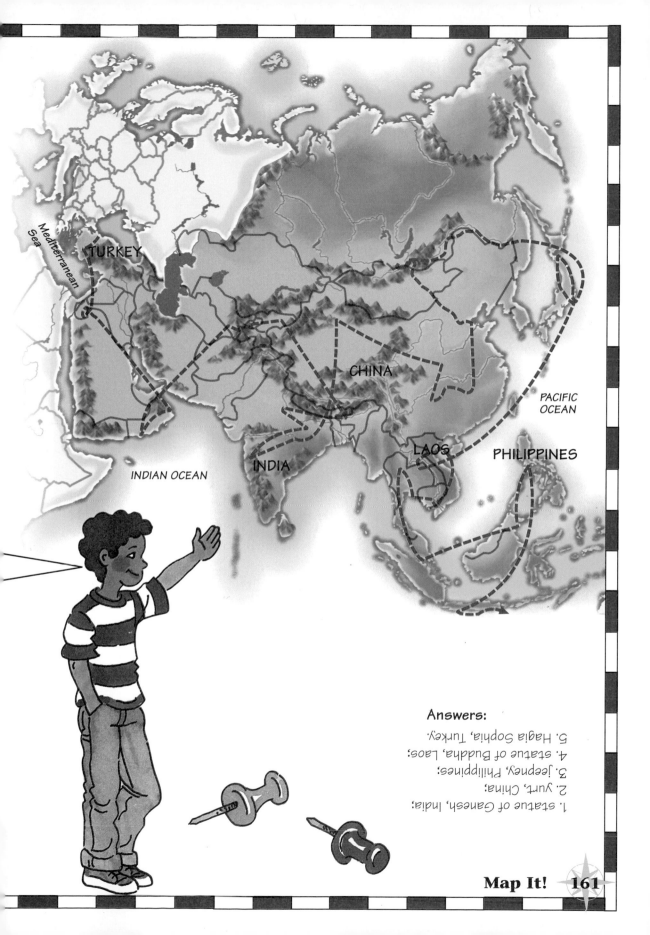

Mediterranean Sea

TURKEY

CHINA

PACIFIC OCEAN

INDIAN OCEAN

INDIA

LAOS

PHILIPPINES

Answers:

1. Statue of Ganesh, India;
2. yurt, China;
3. jeepney, Philippines;
4. Statue of Buddha, Laos;
5. Hagia Sophia, Turkey.

Map It!   **161**

Australia is both a country and a continent. It lies between the South Pacific Ocean and the Indian Ocean. Australia is often called "the land down under" because it lies entirely south of the equator.

Large parts of Australia, especially in the center and the west, are very dry, and not many people live in some areas. Only a few places receive enough rain to support a lot of people.

New Zealand is both a country and a group of islands. The Pacific Islands are a group of thousands of islands scattered across the Pacific Ocean. No one knows for sure exactly how many islands there are. Some of the islands are large, but others are no more than a pile of rocks sticking out of the ocean. The Pacific Islands can be divided into three main areas: Melanesia, Micronesia, and Polynesia.

October 3

From the airplane, we saw that Auckland, New Zealand's largest city, lies on land between two harbors. When we landed, we saw railroads, major roads, and shipyards. This city is a transportation center!

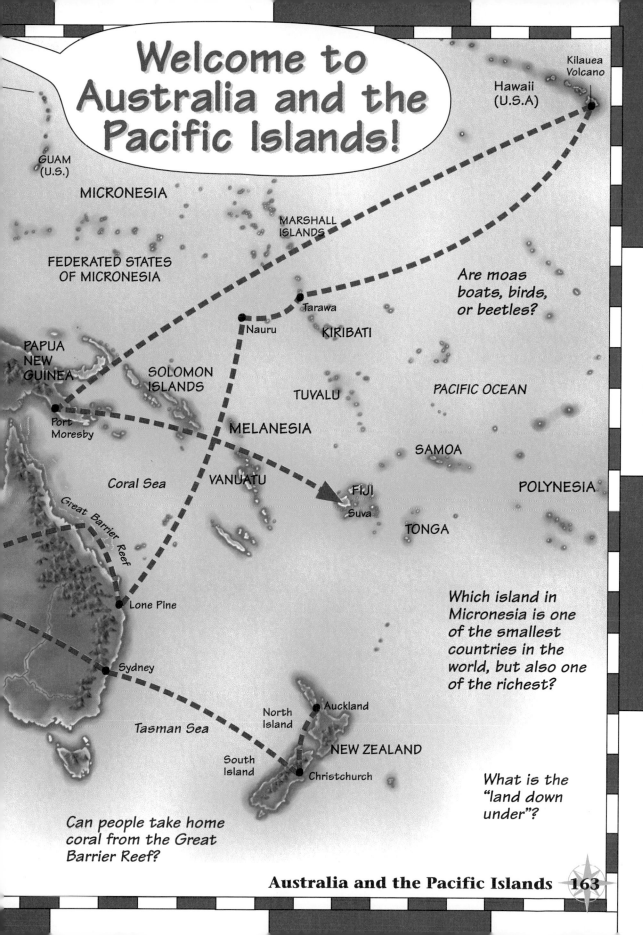

October 4

The Maori (MAH oh ree) were the first people to live in New Zealand. Experts believe they came from nearby islands in canoes, probably more than 1,000 years ago. Today we toured the War Memorial Museum in Auckland. Our guide showed us a beautiful collection of Maori arts and handicrafts, including a huge war canoe carved from a single tree.

According to Maori legend, the hero Maui created the North Island by fishing it up from the sea. The Maori lived in New Zealand many years before the first Europeans saw New Zealand in 1642. In 1840, the Maori and Britain signed an agreement that the British could govern and live in New Zealand, but they had to allow the Maori to own and control their lands. But by 1900, British settlers had taken almost everything from the Maori.

October 5

Today we flew to Christchurch on the South Island. The city lies near the east coast in an area called the Canterbury Plains. The land is perfect for growing wheat and oats.

a Maori carving above a cemetery gate in New Zealand

GUIDEBOOK/NEW ZEALAND

The first Maori lived by hunting and fishing. They have been named the moa hunters because they mainly hunted moas, giant birds that could not fly. By the 1700's, no moas were left.

October 6

We rode a tour bus to Lake Tekapo in the mountains of South Island. From there, we took a tour on a "flight-seeing" ski plane. Glaciers have cut through this land, leaving beautiful lakes and rivers. We flew near Mount Cook, New Zealand's highest mountain. My favorite part was touching down on Tasman Glacier. Sunglasses were a must, because the sun reflecting off the ice was so strong.

The lakes in the heart of the South Island are as blue as Yoshi's turquoise necklace. Our pilot said that the melting snow from the glaciers and mountain peaks gives the water its color. She also explained that water from some of New Zealand's rivers is used to make electric power.

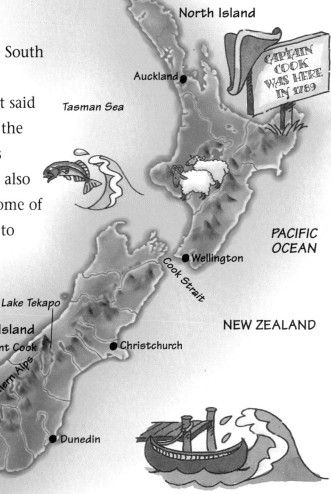

North Island

Auckland

Tasman Sea

CAPTAIN COOK WAS HERE IN 1789

PACIFIC OCEAN

Wellington

Cook Strait

Lake Tekapo

South Island

Mount Cook

Christchurch

NEW ZEALAND

Southern Alps

Dunedin

October 7

G'day mates, from Sydney, Australia's oldest and largest city. We just paid a visit to the Australian Museum. It has lots of information about the Aborigines (AB uh RIHJ uh neez), the first people to live in Australia. We learned that these dark-skinned people have lived in Australia for as long as 50,000 years. British settlers first arrived in 1788. As their settlements grew, they forced many Aborigines from their homes and stole their land. Today, though many Aborigines live in cities, others live in tribal homelands and follow their own way of life.

October 9

In pictures, Ayers Rock looks like a huge, smooth red stone, but it's actually covered with holes, caves, and overhangs. We took a guided walk, a 5.5-mile hike around the entire rock. Our guide was an Aborigine. He pointed out Aboriginal artwork

inside the caves and told us how the rock has special meaning to his people. Their name for Ayers Rock is Uluru. Later we watched the sun set against Uluru. What a sight! As the last rays of the sun struck, the rock seemed to light up from the inside. It absolutely glowed. Just as quickly, the light went out.

October 10

The Great Barrier Reef along Australia's northeast coast is the world's largest group of coral reefs. We took a boat from Cairns to the reef. Our guide told us that the reef is formed by tiny animals called coral polyps. As they grow, they make coverings of limestone. When they die, their coverings become part of the reef. More polyps grow on the limestone and build new layers of reef.

an Aborigine inside a cave
at Ayers Rock

GUIDEBOOK/AUSTRALIA

The Great Barrier Reef is a marine park. Removing living or dead coral, shells, wildlife, or any other part of the reef is a crime.

October 11

We took a boat down the Brisbane River to Lone Pine Koala Sanctuary. This may be our favorite stop on this whole trip! Why? Because we got to see a koala up close! The gray fur ball clutched the guide with his little paws! It was feeding time. As soon as the koalas smelled the fresh eucalyptus leaves, they were wide awake. The guide said koalas rest or sleep up to 19 hours a day.

Tasmanian devils like to eat the remains of dead animals, including the bones.

We had the hardest time leaving the koalas. But when we did, we hand-fed kangaroos, and we saw bandicoots, Tasmanian devils, kookaburras, quolls, and other Australian wildlife. We took pictures to help us remember them all.

Koalas are not bears at all. They are marsupials, mammals that give birth to tiny, poorly developed young. The babies of most marsupials grow bigger and stronger inside a pouch on the mother's belly.

Bandicoots are ratlike marsupials that eat mostly insects, spiders, and worms.

The kookaburra is one of Australia's best known birds, with a call that sounds like someone laughing.

Quolls are spotted marsupials that eat chiefly insects.

The kangaroo is the world's largest marsupial.

At lunch, we wondered why Australia's wildlife is so different from that of any other place. During an animal chat at Lone Pine, a guide explained that at one time all the continents were part of one huge land mass. Australia became separated from this land mass millions and millions of years ago. So its animals developed differently from those on other continents.

Phosphate Mining Taking Its Toll on Nauru

Phosphate mining has had some bad effects on Nauru. To get to the phosphates, workers had to remove the plants. Over time, this has left the land with a bald top. The ground is now so hot that it heats the air overhead like an oven. Few clouds can form in the hot, dry air, so there is little rain, and new plants cannot grow. The government is investigating ways to fix this problem.

October 12

This morning we flew to Nauru (NAH roo). The first Europeans to visit here called it Pleasant Island because the land was so beautiful. This small island country in the central Pacific Ocean is part of Micronesia. It is the third smallest country in the world, yet it is one of the richest. Nauru has made money from phosphates—chemicals used in making fertilizers. Farmers use fertilizers to help crops grow better. But there are limited amounts of phosphates on the island. The people of Nauru have been planning new ways to make money once the phosphates are gone.

PHRASE BOOK

Micronesia means "tiny islands."
Polynesia means "many islands."

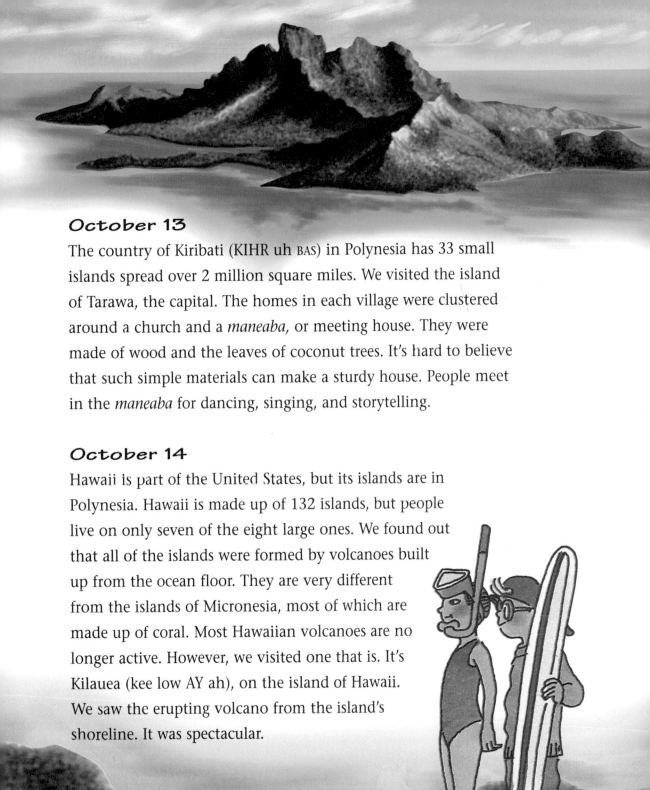

October 13

The country of Kiribati (KIHR uh BAS) in Polynesia has 33 small islands spread over 2 million square miles. We visited the island of Tarawa, the capital. The homes in each village were clustered around a church and a *maneaba,* or meeting house. They were made of wood and the leaves of coconut trees. It's hard to believe that such simple materials can make a sturdy house. People meet in the *maneaba* for dancing, singing, and storytelling.

October 14

Hawaii is part of the United States, but its islands are in Polynesia. Hawaii is made up of 132 islands, but people live on only seven of the eight large ones. We found out that all of the islands were formed by volcanoes built up from the ocean floor. They are very different from the islands of Micronesia, most of which are made up of coral. Most Hawaiian volcanoes are no longer active. However, we visited one that is. It's Kilauea (kee low AY ah), on the island of Hawaii. We saw the erupting volcano from the island's shoreline. It was spectacular.

October 15

We flew into Port Moresby, the capital of Papua New Guinea, a country of Melanesia. Most of the people who live here are Melanesians. We found out that *Melanesia* means "black islands." Its name comes from the word *melanin*, which is a blackish chemical made in the skin. The Melanesian people have large amounts of melanin in their skin. That's what makes their skin so dark.

As we drove to the Highlands of Papua New Guinea, our guide told us that the area was hidden

These Melanesian children in Papua New Guinea are dressed in traditional clothes.

from outsiders for years and years. No one dreamed that anyone lived in the towering, mist-covered mountains. Then, in the 1930's, prospectors went looking for gold and discovered that thousands of people were living there. The people they met had elaborately decorated bodies and wore feathers of the bird of paradise. Today, the Highlanders still decorate themselves with face paint, feathers, shells, and wigs.

birds of paradise

October 16

Our last stop in Melanesia was Fiji, a country of more than 300 islands. The people here are so friendly! Fijians still follow many of their old customs. Most live in tribes in small villages and grow food for their families on land owned by the tribe.

On our tour of Suva, the capital, we learned that almost half of Fiji's people are Indians. Beginning in 1879, they came from India to work the sugar-cane fields. They agreed to work for five years. Many of them stayed, rented land, and became farmers. Today many Indians own businesses.

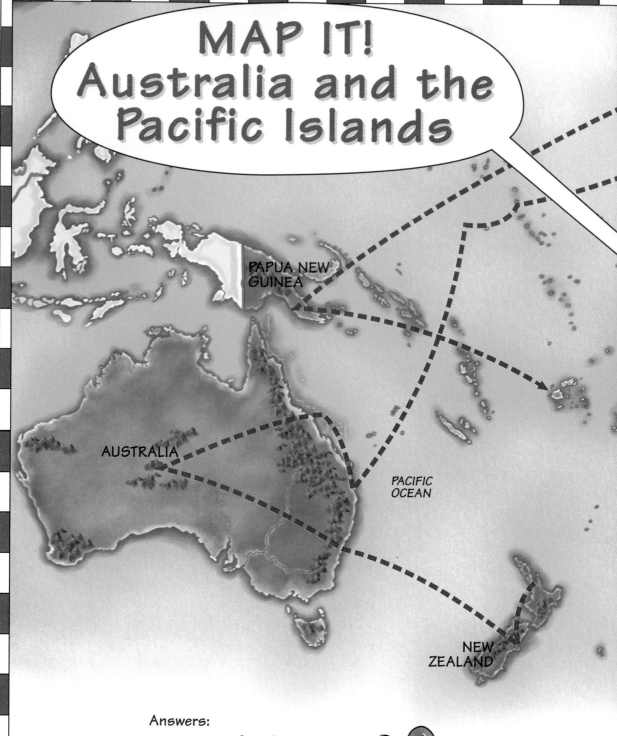

MAP IT!
Australia and the Pacific Islands

PAPUA NEW GUINEA

AUSTRALIA

PACIFIC OCEAN

NEW ZEALAND

Answers:
1. traditional clothes, Papua New Guinea;
2. moa, New Zealand;
3. Maori carving, New Zealand;
4. bird-of-paradise feathers, Papua New Guinea;
5. baby kangaroo, Australia.

We did it. We traveled all the way across Australia and the Pacific Islands. See the giant thumbtacks on this page? Inside each one is a picture clue of one of our favorite places in Australia and the Pacific Islands. If the thumbtacks were real, could you pin each one correctly on the map to show in which country the pictured place is? We drew the route to remind you of where our travels took us.

1. worn by many people

2. all gone

3. guards a gate

4. worn for decoration

5. the ride's on Mom

Onward, Africa! Africa is the second largest continent in the world. It has more land and more people than any continent except Asia. It is home to the world's largest desert and the world's longest river. Most of Africa is a large, flat plateau with narrow coastal plains. Deserts and a few mountain ranges divide the land.

Southern Africa is rich in wildlife, minerals, and history. So we decided to begin our trip there.

October 17

We flew into Johannesburg, South Africa, at dusk. It sparkled with city lights. I thought Africa would be all forest and grassland, but Johannesburg, with its suburbs, has about 2 million people. It's one of the fastest-growing cities in the world!

Would rhinos be safer from hunters if they didn't have horns?

The people of Africa speak more than 800 different languages. How do they manage to communicate?

Are gold mines shiny inside?

Welcome to Southern Africa!

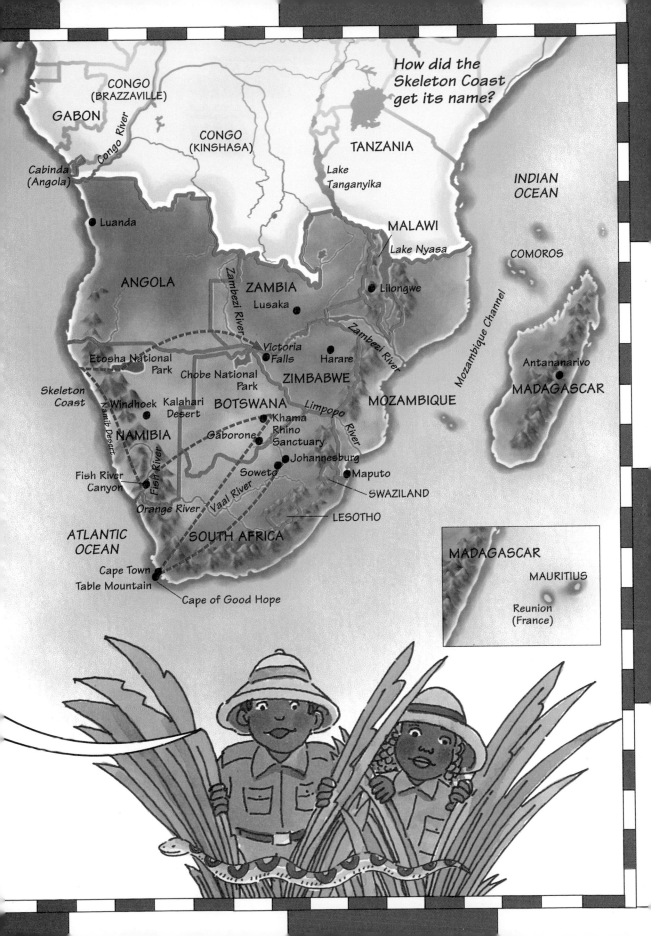

How did the Skeleton Coast get its name?

GABON

CONGO (BRAZZAVILLE)

CONGO (KINSHASA)

TANZANIA

Congo River

Cabinda (Angola)

Luanda

ANGOLA

Lake Tanganyika

MALAWI

Lake Nyasa

INDIAN OCEAN

COMOROS

ZAMBIA

Lusaka

Lilongwe

Zambezi River

Etosha National Park

Victoria Falls

Harare

Zambezi River

Mozambique Channel

Antananarivo

MADAGASCAR

Skeleton Coast

Chobe National Park

ZIMBABWE

MOZAMBIQUE

Windhoek

Kalahari Desert

BOTSWANA

Limpopo River

Namib Desert

NAMIBIA

Gaborones

Khama Rhino Sanctuary

Johannesburg

Maputo

Fish River Canyon

Fish River

Soweto

SWAZILAND

Orange River

Vaal River

LESOTHO

ATLANTIC OCEAN

SOUTH AFRICA

MADAGASCAR

MAURITIUS

Cape Town
Table Mountain

Reunion (France)

Cape of Good Hope

October 18

Johannesburg is the "City of Gold." It began as a gold-mining town. We spent most of the morning at nearby Gold Reef City. The mine here was once the richest gold mine in the world. Now it's a living museum.

We wandered through the old-time streets, and our tour guide taught us one of the old gumboot dances the miners used to do.

October 19

Near Johannesburg is the Lesedi Cultural Village. It's a village where Zulu, Xhosa, Pedi, and Sotho people live. They live in traditional houses and show visitors their traditional ways of living, farming, and herding animals.

Some of the families invited us to have lunch. This was our yummy menu:

Chicken stew
Pap—a porridge made of ground corn.
Mealies—roasted sweet corn.
Vegetables—spinach, beans, and pumpkin.

Tonight, we've been invited to join in some traditional dancing, singing, and storytelling. We can't wait!

GUIDEBOOK/SOUTH AFRICA

Gold and diamond mines are dark and dirty. The gold and diamonds don't shine much at all at first. After gold is mined and refined, it glows!

October 20

We were excited to visit Soweto. For nearly 50 years, until the early 1990's, the government of South Africa had a policy called apartheid. During that time, black people were not allowed to live in the same areas with white people. Most black people in Johannesburg had to live in the Southwestern Townships. They called the area Soweto for short. Soweto had few city services, and many of the people were very poor. But the people of Soweto didn't let that defeat them. Our bus driver showed us a picture of Nelson Mandela. He said that Mandela and others worked to build a community. That community fought for—and helped win—equal rights for all South Africans. We all cheered when our bus driver pointed out the house where Mandela once lived.

Nelson Mandela, far right, at home in Soweto

Southern Africa 179

Table Mountain

October 22

This morning, we rode a cable car up Table Mountain, just outside Cape Town. It's so lush! Table Mountain has more plant species than all of the United Kingdom. Thank goodness we arrived before the rainy season. A park ranger told us it rains buckets!

The ranger also told us about the stars that are visible here in the Southern Hemisphere. She showed us how to find the Southern Cross. We can't wait for night, so that we can go outside and try to find some of the constellations on our own!

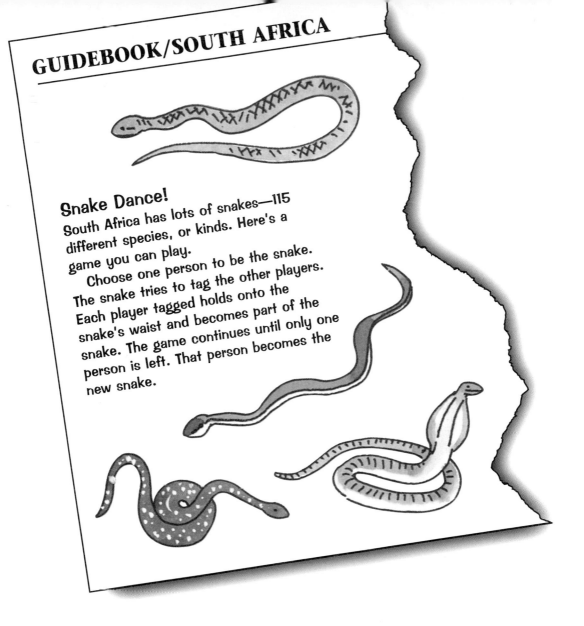

Snake Dance!

South Africa has lots of snakes—115 different species, or kinds. Here's a game you can play.

Choose one person to be the snake. The snake tries to tag the other players. Each player tagged holds onto the snake's waist and becomes part of the snake. The game continues until only one person is left. That person becomes the new snake.

October 24

Yesterday we flew into Botswana. Our favorite spot, so far, is the Khama Rhino Sanctuary. The rangers here are breeding and protecting wild rhinos to try to save them from extinction. Rhino horns are still in demand because some people think they have healing powers. People even use the horns to try to make magic. So these rangers have a big job ahead of them!

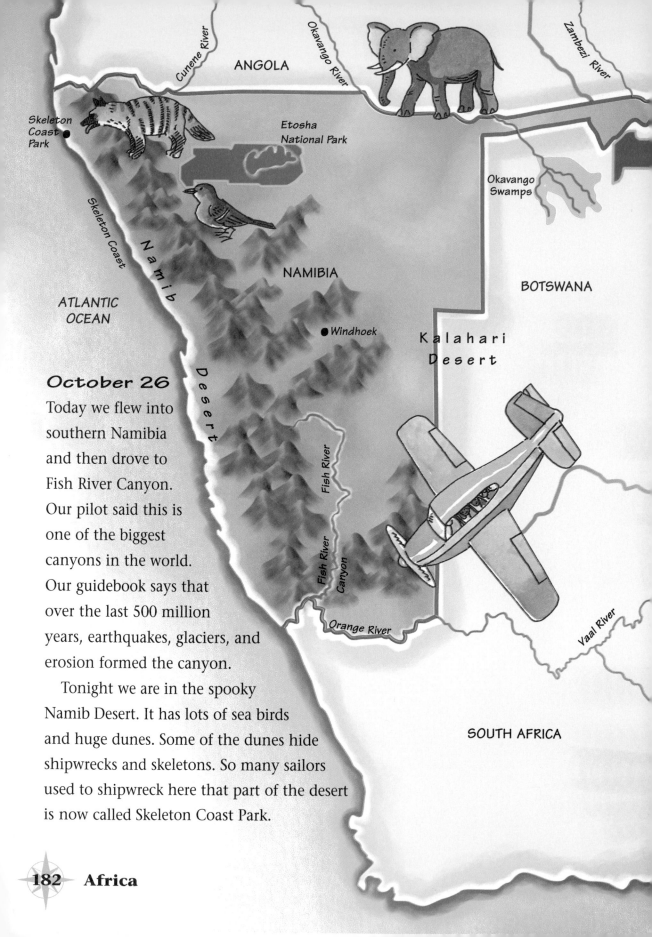

ANGOLA

Cunene River

Okavango River

Zambezi River

Skeleton
Coast
Park

Etosha
National Park

Okavango
Swamps

Skeleton Coast

Namib

ATLANTIC
OCEAN

NAMIBIA

BOTSWANA

Windhoek

Kalahari
Desert

Desert

Fish River

Fish River

Fish River
Canyon

Orange River

Vaal River

SOUTH AFRICA

October 26
Today we flew into
southern Namibia
and then drove to
Fish River Canyon.
Our pilot said this is
one of the biggest
canyons in the world.
Our guidebook says that
over the last 500 million
years, earthquakes, glaciers, and
erosion formed the canyon.

Tonight we are in the spooky
Namib Desert. It has lots of sea birds
and huge dunes. Some of the dunes hide
shipwrecks and skeletons. So many sailors
used to shipwreck here that part of the desert
is now called Skeleton Coast Park.

ZAMBIA

Lake Kariba

Victoria
Falls

Chobe National Park

ZIMBABWE

October 28

We're staying at Etosha National Park in Namibia, near a water hole that's lighted at night. We can watch elephants and other animals that come here after dark to drink.

Millions of years ago, Etosha Pan was an inland sea. Over the years, the sea shrank. Today, it is home to antelope, black rhino, cheetah, elephant, giraffe—we think there's an animal for every letter of the alphabet!

October 30

We have never seen people more beautifully dressed than the Herero women of Namibia and Botswana. They wear long, colorful skirts, and headdresses that are folded to look like a bull's horns. German missionaries in the 1800's gave Herero women full skirts, wide blouses, and headdresses. They used the styles but made new designs.

These Herero women are carrying pails on their heads.

November 3

We thought we knew Victoria Falls because we had seen it in a movie. But there is nothing like feeling the spray as you walk across one of the largest waterfalls in the world.

Eastern Africa is a land of discovery. It includes grasslands and mountains, valleys and lakes, and famous Mount Kilimanjaro. It is home to lions, gazelles, and mountain gorillas. Traditional hunters and farmers live and work in eastern Africa. So do modern city dwellers.

Eastern Africa also is home of some of the world's greatest discoveries, such as *Homo habilis,* an early tool-using human. These discoveries have earned the area a nickname as the "cradle of humanity."

What endangered animals can be seen in eastern Africa?

Who lives in eastern Africa today?

What is a matatu? Do you eat it, ride in it, or wear it?

November 5

Early this morning we boarded a small plane to Tanzania (tan zuh NEE uh). On the way, we got to see Lake Nyasa from the air. It is almost as long as the country of Malawi! This afternoon, we landed in Dar es Salaam, Tanzania's capital city. Now we're going shopping for supplies. We're going to be out in the wild a lot!

Welcome to Eastern Africa!

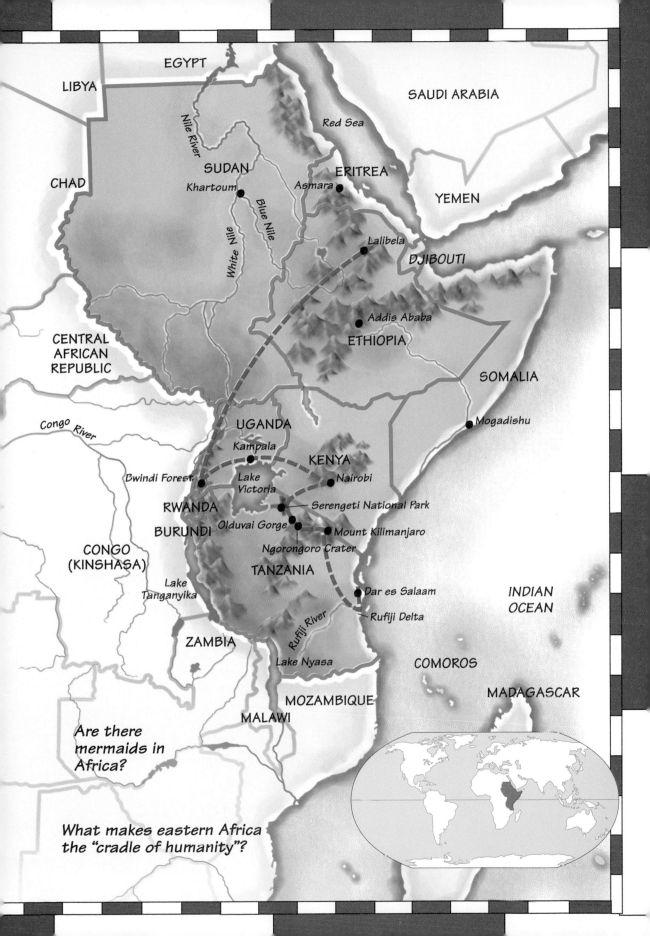

EGYPT

LIBYA

CHAD

SUDAN

Nile River

Khartoum

White Nile   *Blue Nile*

CENTRAL
AFRICAN
REPUBLIC

SAUDI ARABIA

Red Sea

ERITREA

Asmara

YEMEN

Lalibela

DJIBOUTI

Addis Ababa

ETHIOPIA

SOMALIA

Congo River

UGANDA

Kampala

KENYA

Nairobi

Mogadishu

Bwindi Forest

Lake
Victoria

RWANDA

BURUNDI

Serengeti National Park

Olduvai Gorge

Mount Kilimanjaro

Ngorongoro Crater

CONGO
(KINSHASA)

Lake
Tanganyika

TANZANIA

Dar es Salaam

INDIAN
OCEAN

Rufiji Delta

Rufiji River

ZAMBIA

Lake Nyasa

COMOROS

MADAGASCAR

MOZAMBIQUE

MALAWI

Are there mermaids in Africa?

What makes eastern Africa the "cradle of humanity"?

November 6

We learned the legend of the baobab. Baobab trees live up to 2,000 years. They have thick trunks and short branches, and they grow to be enormous. Some people say that the first baobab trees would not stay still. So God replanted them upside down, and they remain that way today.

November 7

Today we saw the mermaids of the Rufiji Delta. They're not really mermaids—they're sea creatures like manatees. But they do use their fins like arms. And when they dive, their tails look like mermaid tails. We rode in a dhow, a small wooden ship with triangular sails. People have sailed dhows along the coasts of eastern Africa, Arabia, and India for hundreds of years. Some of them have a motor, but we only used a sail.

GUIDEBOOK/EASTERN AFRICA

Here are some quick tips for getting the most out of your animal-watching:

* Begin your trip when animals start hunting, in the early morning or late afternoon.
* Ride slowly and quietly. Look on the ground and in the branches overhead.
* In grasslands, keep an eye out for vultures gathering in the branches of a tree.
* In wooded areas, listen for noisy monkeys and baboons. They're probably excited about a nearby leopard.
* Keep a respectful distance from the animals. If they seem nervous, back away.

We're at Mount Kilimanjaro National Park—home to giraffes, lions, leopards, and more. The two peaks of Kilimanjaro are called Kibo and Mawensi. Kibo, the higher one, is always covered with ice and snow.

November 8

Today we drove to the Ngorongoro crater. Our guide said it was once a volcano, probably the size of Kilimanjaro. Then it collapsed. It left a crater and a lake that are now filled with wildlife. Some people call it "Paradise on Earth."

It didn't seem like paradise for the animals, though. It was crawling with buses, jeeps, and tourists. We were glad to leave for the quiet of nearby Olduvai Gorge.

November 8

We rode to Olduvai Gorge, in Africa's Great Rift Valley. On the way, our guide told us that the earth's crust in this area is actually pulling apart, creating volcanoes, lakes, and some of Africa's greatest scenery.

GUIDEBOOK/OLDUVAI GORGE

Imagine the thrill of finding human remains from more than a million years ago. That happened right here, when scientist Mary Leakey discovered the jaw of Nutcracker Man, who lived more than a million years ago.

Louis Leakey discovered another early human in the same spot. We call him Homo Habilis, the tool user. Here is what he may have looked like.

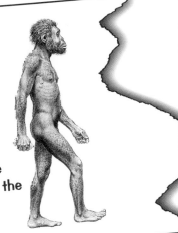

Masai women in Kenya wear beautiful fabrics and beads.

November 12

Poachers are a big problem in Eastern Africa. Today we talked to members of a poaching patrol in the Serengeti National Park. They told us that their job is to protect the animals, watch for poachers, and keep the fences in good shape. We're glad we didn't see any people with guns!

November 15

Tradition is alive and well in Kenya! More than 70 tribal groups live here, and many are hunters, ranchers, craftspeople, and farmers.

Many of the Masai and Samburu people live as nomads, traveling from place to place herding cattle. We saw some Masai with their cattle. The Luo live by fishing and farming. Kalenjin tribes include hunters and farmers. The Akamba have been traders for hundreds of years.

Many people here do some trading. We could hardly believe the beautiful crafts we saw for sale.

Yoshi bought her mom a kanga, a colorful wrap-around dress. Gabe got his dad a beautiful, strong basket made of wood from the baobab tree. Julia got an "elephant hair" bracelet for her sister once she learned it was woven from plastic fishing line! And Steven bought a teeny carved soapstone elephant to remind him of this trip to Africa.

Although the people we met were from many tribes and spoke many

Jambo means "hello" in Swahili.
Karibu means "welcome."

languages, we found out that most of them also speak Swahili. Here in east Africa, it's the language that many tribes use to do business.

November 20

In Nairobi, Kenya, today we found instant adventure. We rode to our hotel in a matatu. That's a vanlike taxi. Ours had a fast, fearless driver. We almost fell off our seats! Our next adventure was at lunch. We had munchable bugs—locusts, grasshoppers, and queen termites, roasted and raw!

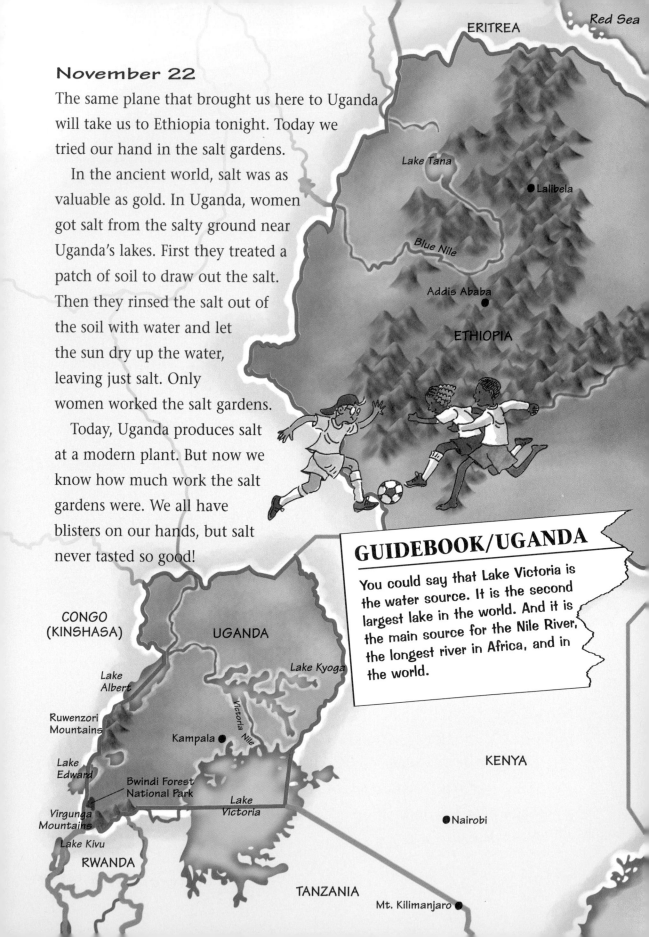

November 22

The same plane that brought us here to Uganda will take us to Ethiopia tonight. Today we tried our hand in the salt gardens.

In the ancient world, salt was as valuable as gold. In Uganda, women got salt from the salty ground near Uganda's lakes. First they treated a patch of soil to draw out the salt. Then they rinsed the salt out of the soil with water and let the sun dry up the water, leaving just salt. Only women worked the salt gardens.

Today, Uganda produces salt at a modern plant. But now we know how much work the salt gardens were. We all have blisters on our hands, but salt never tasted so good!

ERITREA

Red Sea

Lake Tana

● Lalibela

Blue Nile

Addis Ababa ●

ETHIOPIA

GUIDEBOOK/UGANDA

You could say that Lake Victoria is the water source. It is the second largest lake in the world. And it is the main source for the Nile River, the longest river in Africa, and in the world.

CONGO
(KINSHASA)

UGANDA

Lake
Albert

Lake Kyoga

Ruwenzori
Mountains

Victoria Nile

Kampala ●

KENYA

Lake
Edward

Bwindi Forest
National Park

Lake
Victoria

Virgunga
Mountains

● Nairobi

Lake Kivu

RWANDA

TANZANIA

Mt. Kilimanjaro ●

YEMEN

Gulf of Aden

DJIBOUTI

SOMALIA

Wabe Shebele

Eleven of these churches, were built in Lalibela, Ethiopia, in the 1100's and 1200's. Each one was carved from a single piece of red rock!

The rock churches are still used today. Many people come to services there.

Only about 630 mountain gorillas are left in the world. Many of them live here in Uganda and find safety in national parks, such as Bwindi Forest National Park. But money to run the parks is scarce.

November 23

Ethiopia is mostly mountains and highlands, but it borders the Red Sea. Since ancient times, Ethiopians have traded with many other countries. We are on our way to Lalibela to see some old and unusual churches.

Eastern Africa

Western Africa is hot and mostly flat. The Sahara Desert is in the north. South of the Sahara is the Sahel, a dry grassland. Some of it overlaps with the Sahara Desert. Farther south, there are forests and tropical rain forests.

It's cool and dry here from December to February. The harmattan winds break the heat, but they kick up a lot of sand and dust. Some days, there is so much wind and sand that planes are grounded.

November 24

Last night, after a long flight across the Sahel, we landed in Natitingou, in the low mountains of northern Benin.

This morning, we drove to the coast, about 300 miles away. Just before we reached the ocean, we visited the fishing village of Ganvié. It's built over Lake Nokoué, and it's entirely on stilts!

How did Lake Volta get so big?

What's so special about the dolphins in Mauritania?

WESTERN SAHARA

Arguin Bank

MAURITANIA

CAPE VERDE

Senegal River

Dakar

SENEGAL

GAMBIA

GUINEA-BISSAU

GUINEA

Freetown

SIERRA LEONE

ATLANTIC OCEAN

Monrovia

LIBERIA

Kola nuts are tough! How do chimps open them?

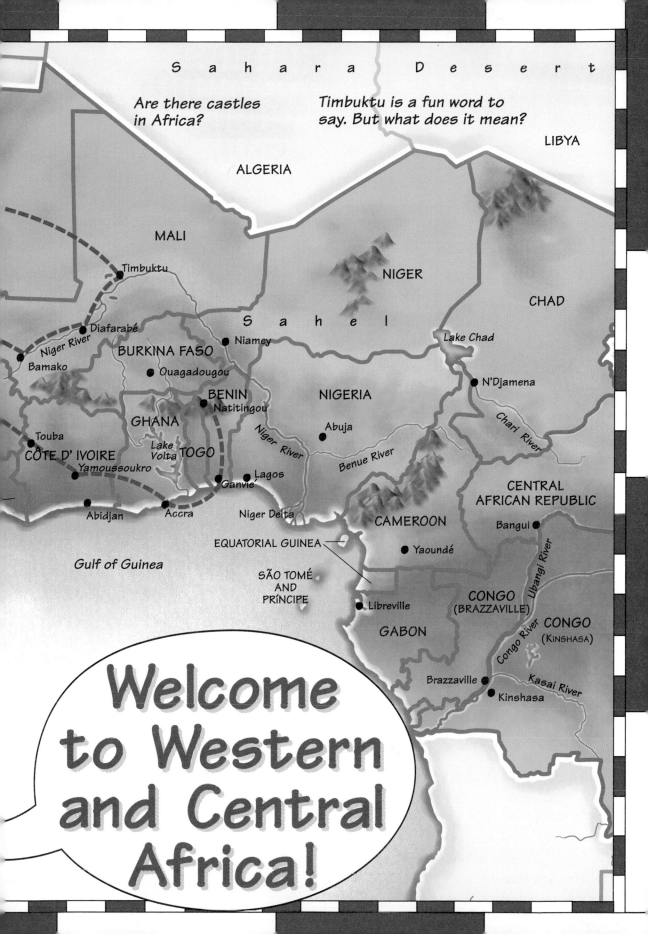

Welcome to Western and Central Africa!

We marveled at this and other beautiful gold carvings in Ghana!

A cannon is aimed out of this castle on the shore of Ghana.

November 26

We sailed to Ghana today, like European traders used to do. High up on a rocky shore stands St. George, Ghana's most famous castle. During colonial times, Europeans used it to store gold and ivory. Other forts and castles also line the shores of Benin and Ghana. Many had a shameful purpose: they held prisoners for the slave trade. Today, most are in ruins.

Mystery solved: the skipper of our boat told us that Lake Volta is artificial! It's made by the Akosombo Dam over the Volta River. The dam supplies Ghana with all its electricity.

November 27

It was exciting to visit an Ashanti market. The Ashanti people of Ghana once were famous for gold. Their king had golden instruments, gold jewelry and decorations, and a dazzling golden stool. Nowadays, Ghana is famous for crafts. The craft village of Ahwiaa is famous for woodcarving. Pankrono is famous for pottery. We saw pottery and stools with amazing carvings of elephants, leopards, and lions. Bonwire is known for kente cloth, woven with beautiful colors and designs. Ntonso is known for adinkra cloth, a kind of cloth with printed symbols that often tell stories.

Lunch was yummy. We tried different soups:

Abankwan—Soup of pounded palm fruit and fish.

Nkatenkwan—Groundnut soup with peanut butter, onions, tomatoes, and meat or fish.

Shito—Pepper soup. The house specialty.

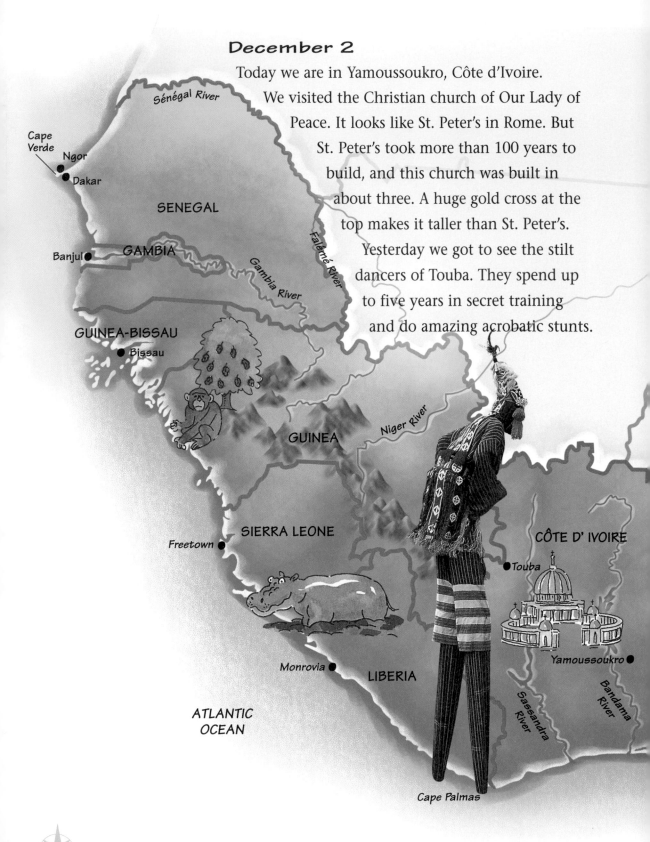

December 2

Today we are in Yamoussoukro, Côte d'Ivoire. We visited the Christian church of Our Lady of Peace. It looks like St. Peter's in Rome. But St. Peter's took more than 100 years to build, and this church was built in about three. A huge gold cross at the top makes it taller than St. Peter's. Yesterday we got to see the stilt dancers of Touba. They spend up to five years in secret training and do amazing acrobatic stunts.

Sénégal River

Cape Verde

Ngor

Dakar

SENEGAL

Falémé River

Banjul

GAMBIA

Gambia River

GUINEA-BISSAU

Bissau

GUINEA

Niger River

SIERRA LEONE

Freetown

CÔTE D' IVOIRE

Touba

Monrovia

LIBERIA

Yamoussoukro

ATLANTIC OCEAN

Sassandra River

Bandama River

Cape Palmas

It's kola nut season. Chimps in the national parks use stones to crack open the nuts and eat them. We really could not see them, but we could hear them!

December 4

Dakar in Senegal may be the most beautiful city in western Africa. It sticks out into the Atlantic Ocean, so the sea is nearly all around us. The city is cool and dry this time of year, but a little dusty from the harmattan.

We spent the day at the beach. Last night, we had poulet yassa, chicken with lemon and onions. It came with millet and vegetables and a red drink made with bissap flowers. Yum!

Dear Jack,
West Africa really swings! They have great instruments, like the kora, which is made from a huge gourd and sounds like a harp. I got tapes of juju music, Makossa music, Nigerian Afro-beat, highlife, and pop music from the Congo. When I get back, we can play some of it.
Bye, Gabe

White Volta

Black Volta

Lake Volta

GHANA

Abidjan

WEST AFRICA

December 7

Africa is so huge! We took the express train from Dakar to Bamako, here in Mali, and it still took two days. But we got to meet lots of people on the train. Many of the people we met are Moors, Muslims who speak Arabic and live in northern or northwestern Africa. They told us that Moors may have Arab, Spanish, Jewish, or Turkish ancestors, and that Moors once ruled an empire that included Spain.

Timbuktu is a sandy town on the outskirts of the Sahara Desert. It was once a major stop on trade routes through the desert. During the reign of Mansa Musa, 100,000 people lived and worked in Timbuktu.

According to one legend, Timbuktu is named after a Tuareg woman who was in charge of the early settlement. Her name—and the name Timbuktu—means "mother with a large navel!"

The sands blew in the Sahara, and we got sand in our sandwiches!

The "Lion King" isn't just a movie or a play about a lion. It is also the name of real person, Sundiata Keita. This lion king founded the Empire of Mali in the 1200's. The popular movie and play are loosely based on his life.

By the 1300's, Mali controlled almost all trade across the Western Sahara. Djenné and Timbuktu became rich from trading in salt, gold, and other goods. Sundiata Keita is still a hero of the Malinke people of West Africa.

December 8

We flew in a bush plane to Diafarabé. We were lucky to get there just in time for the yearly cattle-crossing. It's a tradition in Mali that goes back more than 150 years.

Every year when the dry season begins, the herders drive their cattle from the Sahara to greener pastures across the Niger River. They wait until the river is low enough to cross. On the first day of the crossing, they hold a huge celebration, with music and dancing—and thousands of cows.

a mask made by the Dogon people

December 11

Today we took the bush plane to the town of Sanga. Then we hired a Dogon guide to show us around. He took us through the villages near the town and helped us talk to villagers. Then he led us on a trek around the cliff dwellings where Dogon people once lived. They reminded me of the Pueblo dwellings in North America.

December 13

Hundreds of thousands of birds stop here on their way between Europe, northern Asia, and Africa. We're at Arguin

The long-tailed cormorant has webbed feet and dives for its meals. It is related to the pelican.

Bank, in Mauritania. Small sand islands dot the clear blue sea here. The migrating birds nest and rest on these islands.

Other amazing animals here are the dolphins. You know how sheep dogs round up sheep? Well, these dolphins actually help the Imraguen people round up fish!

Northern Africa is next to the desert, but it also has grasslands, plateaus, valleys, deltas, and shoreline. In the mountains, it sometimes snows. There are basically two seasons—dry and rainy. The Nile River Valley is home to some of the wonders of the world.

The people of northern Africa include Berbers, Arabs, Africans, and Europeans. Many are Muslim, Christian, or Jewish, but many people follow other faiths.

December 14

Our morning flight crossed the Tropic of Cancer. It is the farthest point north at which the sun can shine straight down on the earth. But as we go farther north, the weather still is warm.

During our quick stop on the Canary Islands, we found out that Canaries were first found there and were named for the islands. But the islands were named for dogs! Sailors long ago found fierce dogs there. They called the place *Canaria* from the Latin word for dog.

PORTUGAL SPAIN

ATLANTIC OCEAN

Rabat

Casablanca

Fez

Madeira (Portugal)

MOROCCO

Marrakech

Atlas Mountains

Canary Islands (Spain)

Jebel Toubkal

Las Palmas

WESTERN SAHARA

MAURITANIA

MALI

Welcome to Northern Africa!

ITALY

GREECE

TURKEY

Mediterranean Sea

Algiers

Tunis

MALTA

CYPRUS

SYRIA

TUNISIA

LEBANON

Tripoli

Alexandria

ISRAEL

JORDAN

Cairo

Suez
Canal

ALGERIA

Siwah Oasis

SAUDI
ARABIA

LIBYA

EGYPT

Nile River

Red
Sea

S a h a r a   D e s e r t

Luxor

Aswan

Lake Nasser

NIGER

CHAD

SUDAN

Why is the Nile River
so important to
Egypt?

What kind of
wildlife is special
to Morocco?

Did aliens build the
pyramids of Egypt?

What is the secret
of the sphinx?

December 18

Casablanca is Morocco's largest city. During World War II it was a dangerous place. Part of the war was fought here. Today it has a huge seaport and many businesses. People from many countries come to visit or work here.

We loved the Hassan II Mosque (mahsk). In the 1980's and 1990's, thousands of workers built it. It's one of the largest in the world.

We also visited Fez and Marrakech. Both cities have old walled sections from the Middle Ages. In the old section of Marrakech, there's a suq in the square called Place Djemma el-Fna. We bought couscous from a food stall and ate as snake charmers, acrobats, and jugglers performed. Couscous is steamed ground wheat with vegetables, meat, and broth.

A snake responds to a snake charmer's movements. Sometimes a snake charmer plays music, but the snake does not hear the music.

December 17

We are on a two-day trek in the Atlas Mountains. In the sky, we've seen lots of birds. Many birds fly over Morocco in the spring and fall, when they migrate between Europe and Africa. This afternoon, we went on a mule ride to get a good view of Jebel Toukbal. That's Morocco's highest peak.

December 18

We're in Morocco during the month of Ramadan. During Ramadan, all Muslims fast from dawn until sunset. Only the tourists buy food during the day. But the month will end with big feasts for everyone. Wish we could go to one!

December 20

In Tunis, the capital of Tunisia, many people wear Western clothes and listen to pop music. And we saw some fast-food restaurants. But the countryside of Tunisia is very traditional. Almost every village has a mosque, a bathhouse, and a cafe.

a busy open-air market at Place Djemma el-Fna

PHRASE BOOK

A suq is a marketplace where food and goods are for sale.

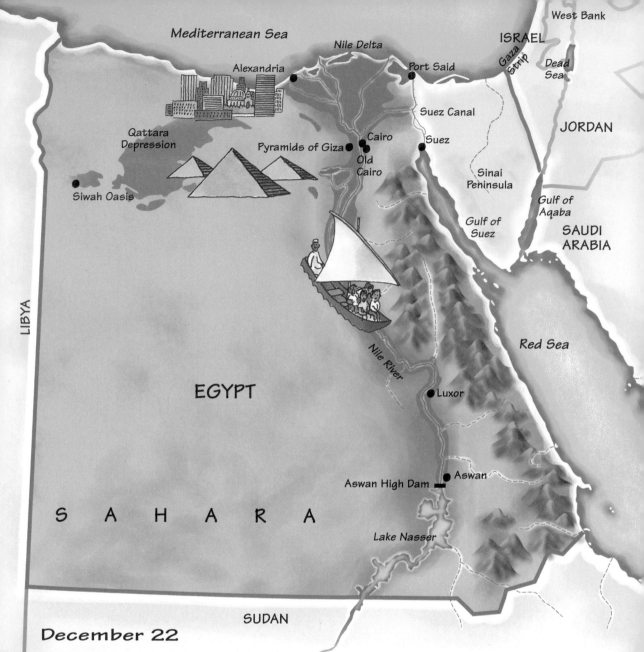

December 22

Alexandria is one of the world's oldest cities. It is also Egypt's chief port city. It is named after Alexander the Great, who founded the city in 331 B.C. People came from all over to visit its library. Its lighthouse was one of the Seven Wonders of the Ancient World.

It is warm here, but there are cool breezes from the sea. What a great place to spend the first day of winter!

December 23

Today we took a tour bus to the Siwah Oasis. An oasis is a place in the desert where underground water comes close to the surface. At Siwah, there are more than 200 springs and hundreds of thousands of palm trees—enough water and plant life for many families. Siwah is famous for its dates, which grow on palm trees.

We saw the temple that holds the Oracle of Amon. Some ancient leaders asked the advice of oracles to help them rule. Legends say this oracle was never wrong.

We did not need the oracle to predict a great trip on the Nile! We booked a felucca, which is a slow-moving sailboat. We sailed from temple to temple. Cotton farmers waved at us from the shore.

Meeting Called to Discuss Dam

Aswan High Dam keeps the Nile from flooding and provides water for crops. But at what cost? Because the Nile no longer floods, it no longer leaves new layers of fertile soil on the land. Farmers grow more crops, but they now need fertilizer. The shores of the river are wearing down, and worms that cause diseases are multiplying.

December 26

Here is the best news yet: We got to meet some of the scientists at Luxor! In 1995, they discovered the largest tomb ever found there. It has more than 100 rooms. The scientists think Ramses II built it for his sons.

The scientists have not found any mummies yet. But they have found pottery, statues, and painted carvings. Some of the carvings show Ramses II presenting his sons to Egyptian gods and goddesses.

The desert has hardly any moisture and no light pollution. So nothing gets in the way of seeing the stars. We never knew there were so many!

Our New Year's resolution is to solve the mystery of the Sphinx. Was it a god or a beast? Who built it—and why?

December 28

Modern Cairo has steel-and-glass buildings, older buildings, and open-air markets. In the south part is Old Cairo. Jewish and Muslim monuments, mosques, and Christian churches stand side by side in peace.

Our favorite thing about Cairo is that it's close to the pyramids at Giza. They're massive! Our guide told us that generations of workers dragged the stone blocks across the desert to build them.

The pyramids were both monuments and tombs. They held the pharaoh's mummy, along with food, drinks, servants, gold, and other treasures.

Not all the ancient tombs were pyramids, though. The Egyptians built other tombs, called *mastabas,* for important people who were not pharaohs. Some were hidden underground.

A Guide to Ancient Gods

The ancient Egyptians worshiped many gods. Here are some of the most important gods:

We made our own miniature pyramids using sugar cubes and glue. Here's how:

1. Make a square base. Glue or paste together 9 rows of 9 sugar cubes.

2. Build upward. For each level, use two fewer sugar cubes on each side. The second level will have 7 rows of 7 cubes, the third level will have 5 rows of 5 cubes, and so on. You can make a bigger pyramid using more cubes, but be sure to begin with an odd number, such as 11 or 13.

3. End with one sugar cube at the top.

Amon-Re sun god. He became the most important god.

Isis wife of Osiris and goddess of bearing young. She brought Osiris back to life after another god killed him.

Osiris god of plants. After Isis saved him, he became god of the underworld and judged people after they died.

Horus son of Isis and Osiris. He conquered the god who had killed Osiris.

MAP IT! Africa

1. buy something beautiful

2. be charming

3. an old-time dance

4. sightseeing with sails

5. a good god who won

We did it. We traveled all the way across another continent—Africa. See the giant thumbtacks on this page? Inside each one is a picture clue of one of our favorite places in Africa.

If the thumbtacks were real, could you pin each one correctly on the map to show in which country the pictured place is? We drew the route to remind you of where our travels took us.

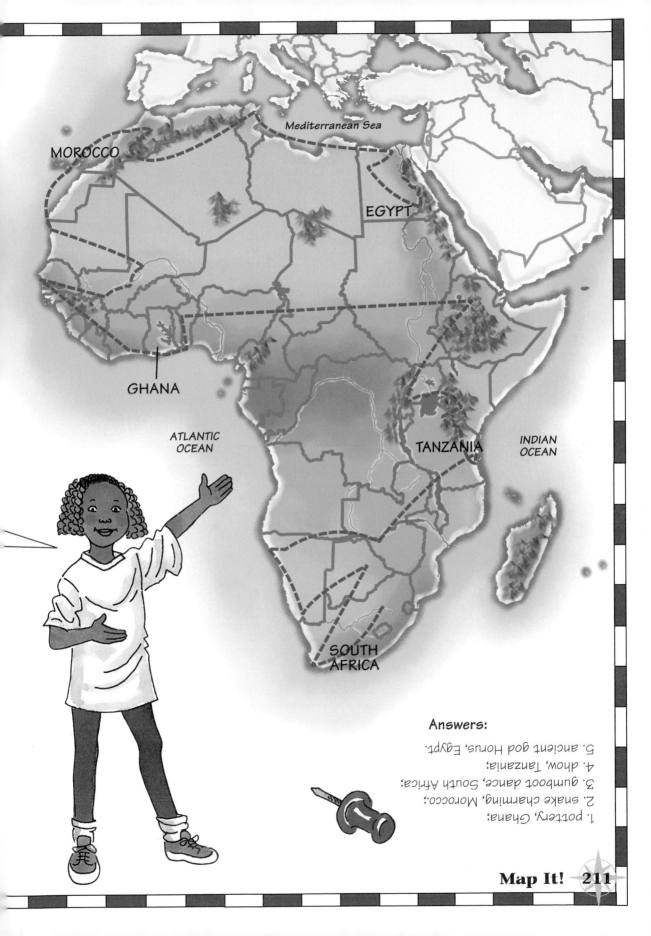

MOROCCO

Mediterranean Sea

EGYPT

GHANA

ATLANTIC
OCEAN

TANZANIA

INDIAN
OCEAN

SOUTH
AFRICA

Answers:

1. pottery, Ghana;
2. snake charming, Morocco;
3. gumboot dance, South Africa;
4. dhow, Tanzania;
5. ancient god Horus, Egypt.

Map It! 211

Welcome Home!

December 29

Have we really been traveling almost a year? It doesn't seem possible—the days went by so fast. Last January, we were on our way to Antarctica. Seven continents and nearly one year later, we are flying home.

While we fly, we're looking at all of our notes and photos and clippings. We are trying to decide which memories of the trip are our favorites. Which are yours?

And what about the foods? Gabe remembers the chivitos, those big steak sandwiches we had in Uruguay. Steve's favorite was the goulash in Hungary.

Crafts? We saw so many beautiful things, and even bought a few of them. Julia loves her delicate ñanduti lace from Paraguay. Yoshi treasures the kanga, the dress she bought in Kenya for her mother.

Places? We saw the Pyramid of the Sun in Mexico and the pyramids at Giza in Egypt. We visited the Forbidden City in Beijing, the Kremlin in Moscow, and the Tower of London. We saw fiords in Norway and icebergs floating in Antarctic waters.

As for the people we met, we'll remember the many different ways they live and how good it was to spend time with them.

We have many exciting things to tell our families and friends. Already we're planning places we'd like to visit on our next world adventure!

Find Out More

There are so many exciting resources for you to use to learn all about people and places around the world. Pick a place or topic, then start your search. You will find plenty to enjoy. The resources listed here are only a sampling. Your school or public library has many more.

Countries

http://www.yahooligans.com/Around_the_World/countries

From this Web site, you can connect to any country in the world, get pictures, maps, and videos of that country. You will also find tons of facts about your country in this awesome site!

Fun on the Run:
Travel Games and Songs

by Joanna Cole and others (Morrow Junior Books, 1999)

This is a collection of games and songs to enjoy while traveling. You and your family will have fun playing word and memory games, license plate games, and more!

GeoTrivia World

by Juliette Underwood (Rand McNally, 1995)

This is the ultimate trivia adventure, covering cities of the world, music, holidays, landmarks, and much, much more. Can you stump your friends?

Greetings from Antarctica

by Sara Wheeler (Peter Bedrich Books, 1999)

The author's letters to her godson and photographs of her expedition to Antarctica will tell you a great deal about this continent. Did you know that six months of the year Antarctica has continuous daylight?

Illustrated Atlas

(World Book, Inc., 1999)

Take a voyage of discovery around the world. Through colorful maps and pictures, find out about the world's lands, plants, animals, people, and industries. Flags of the world's nations are included.

Islands

by Rose Pipes (Raintree Steck-Vaughn, 1999)

Some of the well-known islands of the world are described in this book, including the Maldives, Hawaii, and Madagascar. Other titles in this "World Habitats" series include *Grasslands, Hot Deserts, Rivers and Lakes,* and *Coasts and Shores.*

Kids' Almanac for the 21st Century

by Elaine Pascoe and Deborah Kops (Scholastic, 1999)

As you "travel" around the world, you are sure to have plenty of questions. Try this almanac for some quick-to-find answers.

Our Earth

by Anne Rockwell (Harcourt Brace and Company, 1998)

This book for young readers explains the geography of our Earth. You will be introduced to glaciers, continents, islands, volcanoes, and many other geographic terms.

Picture Reference Atlas

(World Book, Inc., 1996)

Packed with fascinating detail, this book is filled with huge, colorful maps that provide the ideal introduction to the world's countries and continents. Discover places, people, plants, and animals around the globe. Each map has a grid for practicing map-reading skills. Fact Finder questions ask about places on the map. Factfile features provide additional fun.

Road Adventures USA

CD-ROM for Mac and Windows, revised edition (The Learning Company, 2000)

Test your problem-solving skills as you travel across the United States. You will have fun while you read maps, manage a budget, and follow clues to mystery destinations.

Where in the World Is Carmen SanDiego? version 3.5

CD-ROM for Mac and Windows (Broderbund/The Learning Company, 1997)

You will travel to 50 countries, gather clues, and take guided tours to solve cases. Video clips from the National Geographic Society are included.

Glossary

Here are some words you have read in this book. The pronunciation given in parentheses after each word tells you how to say it: archaeological (AHR kee uh LAHJ ih kuhl). Say the parts in small letters in your normal voice, those in small capital letters a little louder, and those in large capital letters loudest. Following the pronunciation are one or two sentences that tell the word's meaning as it is used in this book.

agriculture (AG ruh kuhl chuhr)
The business of farming by planting and raising crops and raising farm animals.

archaeological (AHR kee uh LAHJ ih kuhl)
Having to do with archaeology, the study of the people, customs, and life of ancient times.

canyon (KAN yuhn)
A narrow, deep valley with steep sides.

caravan (KAR uh van)
A group of people, such as traders, who travel together for safety.

cathedral (kuh THEE druhl)
A church that has a high-ranking official, usually a bishop, as its head. Many cathedrals are large and beautiful churches.

civilization (sihv uh luh ZAY shuhn)
A group of people or a nation that has developed its knowledge and way of life very highly. One important civilization was that of the ancient Egyptians.

climate (KLY miht)
The weather that an area has over many years. Many tropical lands have a warm, wet climate.

colony (KAHL uh nee)
A land that is ruled by a far-off country. Often the ruling country sends some people to settle there.

conservation (KAHN suhr VAY shuhn)
Protecting forests, rivers, and other natural areas. Often the animals that live in those areas are also protected.

continent (KAHN tuh nuhnt)
One of the seven large areas of land on the earth. Most of the continents are surrounded or almost surrounded by water.

crater (KRAY tuhr)
The bowl-shaped opening in the top of a volcano.

delta (DEHL tuh)
Soil and sand that washes down a river and forms new land at its mouth. A delta often has three sides, like a triangle.

distribution (DIHS truh BYOO shuhn)
Getting food or goods from

farms and factories to the people who buy them.

dune (doon)
A hill or ridge of loose sand piled up by the wind. Dunes often form on ocean shores and in deserts.

environmentalist (ehn VY ruhn MEHN tuhl ihst)
A person who is concerned about problems with air, water, soil, and living things, including problems such as pollution.

equinox (EE kwuh nahks)
The time twice a year when the earth's equator is directly beneath the sun, and day and night are the same length. The times are about March 21 and September 23.

erosion (ih ROH zhuhn)
The wearing away of rocks or soil. Erosion can be caused by such things as water and wind.

eruption (ih RUHP shuhn)
The act of exploding or bursting out. Gases, ash, cinders, or lava may burst from a volcano during an eruption.

export (ehk SPAWRT)
To send goods to another country to sell.

fortress (FAWR trihs)
A place built with walls and other things that help to protect it from enemies.

gorge (gawrj)
A narrow, deep valley. It is usually rocky and often has a stream.

harmattan (HAHR muh TAN)
A very dry, dusty wind that blows over the Sahara.

herpetologist (HUR puh TAHL uh jihst)
Someone who studies reptiles, such as snakes, and amphibians, such as frogs.

immigrant (IHM uh gruhnt)
A person who comes from another country to live.

import (ihm PAWRT)
To bring goods from another country to sell.

irrigation (IHR uh GAY shuhn)
Using ditches, pipes, pumps, or other systems to bring water to dry land.

longitude (LAHN jih tood)
The distance east or west on the earth's surface. Longitude is measured from an imaginary line that runs from the North to the South Pole and passes through Greenwich, England.

majolica (muh JAHL uh kuh)
A kind of pottery or tile decorated with brightly painted designs.

migrate (MY grayt)
To go from one place to another as the seasons change. Many birds migrate.

mosaic (moh ZAY ihk)
A picture or decoration made of small pieces of stone laid close together and fixed in place with cement.

mosque (mahsk)
A place of worship for Muslims.

naturalist (NACH uhr uh lihst)
A person who studies animals and plants, especially in the places where they live.

navigable (NAV uh guh buhl)
Deep enough and wide enough to be traveled on by boat.

nomad (NOH mad)
A person who belongs to a group that travels from place to place to find food for themselves or their animals.

oasis (oh AY sihs)
A place in the desert where there is water and trees and other plants can grow.

oracle (AWR uh kuhl)
A place where a god or goddess is believed to answer people's questions by speaking through a priest or priestess.

pass (pas)
A narrow road or path through the mountains.

plateau (pla TOH)
A large, flat area of land that is higher than the land around it.

poacher (POH chuhr)
A person who hunts or captures animals that are protected by law.

possession (puh ZEHSH uhn)
An area of land that is ruled by another country.

province (PRAHV uhns)
A large area of a country that has its own government. Canada and some other countries have provinces.

Ramadan (RAM uh dahn)
A holy month in Islam. During Ramadan, Muslims do not eat between sunrise and sunset.

reservoir (REHZ uhr vwahr)
A place where water is collected to use for farming or drinking. Some reservoirs are made by building a dam on a river.

Sahel (suh HEHL)
A large, dry grassland south of the Sahara Desert. In some years, the Sahel is too dry for farming.

silt (sihlt)
Very small bits of soil, sand, or clay that are carried by flowing water.

species (SPEE sheez)
A group of plants or animals that are alike. Members of the same species, such as house cats, can reproduce together.

territory (TEHR uh tawr ee)
An area of land that belongs to a nation. Canada has both provinces and territories.

volcano (vahl KAY noh)
An opening in the earth's crust through which steam, gas, ashes, rocks, and lava burst. Often the volcano forms a mountain as rocks and other matter pile up.

Index

This index is an alphabetical list of important topics covered in this book. It will help you find information given in both words and pictures. To help you understand what an entry means, there is sometimes a helping word in parentheses, for example, **abankwan soup** (food). If there is information in both words and pictures, you will see the words *with pictures* in parentheses after the page number. If there is only a picture, you will see the word *picture* in parentheses after the page number.

Illustration Credits

The publishers of *Childcraft* gratefully acknowledge the courtesy of **George Ulrich** for the illustrations, **Paul Perreault** for the maps, and the following photographers, agencies, and organizations for the photographic illustrations in this volume. When all the illustrations for a sequence of pages are from a single source, the inclusive page numbers are given. Credits should be read from left to right, top to bottom, on their respective pages. All illustrations are the exclusive property of the publishers of *Childcraft* unless names are marked with an asterisk (*).

8-9 © Superstock*; © Robert Frerck, Tony Stone Images*

18-19 © Superstock*

20-21 © J. Drew, TRIP*; © Timothy O'Keefe, Bruce Coleman Inc.*

22-23 © Eitan Simanor, Bruce Coleman Inc.*

26-27 © Jose Fuste Raga, The Stock Market*; © Robert Frerck, Tony Stone Images*

30-31 © Aleiandro Balaguer, Tony Stone Images*; WORLD BOOK photo;

32-33 © Frans Lanting, Photo Researchers*

34-35 © David Rentz, Bruce Coleman Inc.*; © Ulrike Welsch, Photo Researchers*

38-39 © Will & Deni McIntyre, Tony Stone Images*

42-43 WORLD BOOK photo; © Eitan Simanor, Bruce Coleman Inc.*

44-45 © David Dennis, Tom Stack & Associates*

48-49 © Kevin West, Liaison Agency*

50-51 © Don Goode, Photo Researchers*

52-53 WORLD BOOK illustration by Arthur Singer; © Michael Fogden, Earth Scenes*; WORLD BOOK illustration by Robert Kuhn

54-55 © Robert Lubeck, Earth Scenes*; © Norbert Wu, Tony Stone Images*; © Robert Lubeck, Earth Scenes*

56-57 © Steve Vidler, Tony Stone Images*; © Will & Deni McIntyre, Photo Researchers*

60-61 © Superstock*; National Park Service*; © Tony Stone Images*

62-63 © Carol Lewis, Starlight Visitors Association*

66-67 © Hugh Sitton, Tony Stone Images*; © Breck P. Kent, Earth Scenes*

68-69 © Superstock*

74-75 © Howard Buffett*

76-77 © AP/Wide World*; © William H. Mullins, Photo Researchers*

78-79 © Steve Vidler, Tony Stone Images*

80-81 © Ralph Reinhold, Earth Scenes*; © Zig Leszczynski, Animals Animals*

82-83 © Don Goode, Photo Researchers*; © Superstock*; © Tony Stone Images*; © Will & Deni McIntyre, Photo Researchers*

86-87 © Trinity College, Dublin, Ireland/ET Archive, London from Superstock*

88-89 Beatrix Potter*; National Portrait Gallery, Andrew W. Mellon Collection, Washington, DC.*; © Superstock*

90-91 © Superstock*

92-93 © Henri Veller/Explorer from Photo Researchers*; © S. L. Craig, Jr., Bruce Coleman Inc.*; © Dana Hyde, Photo Researchers*; © David R. Frazier*

94-95 © Guido Cozzi, Bruce Coleman Inc.*; © SPL from Photo Researchers*

96-97 ©Superstock*; © Nicholas DeVore III, Bruce Coleman Inc.*; © Massimo Borchi, Bruce Coleman Inc.*; © John Verde, Photo Researchers*

98-99 © Superstock*; © David R. Frazier*

100-101 © John Elk, Bruce Coleman Inc.*

102-103 © Travelpix from FPG*; © Superstock*; © Desjardins/Rapho from Photo Researchers*

104-105 © Desjardins/Rapho from Photo Researchers*

108-109 © Detlev Van Ravensway/SPL from Researchers*; © Jay Pasachoff*; © Louis Goldman, Photo Researchers*; © Superstock*

110-111 © Richard Bergman, Photo Researchers*

112-113 © Superstock*

114-115 © Alan L. Detrick, Photo Researchers*; WORLD BOOK illustration by Kate Lloyd-Jones, Linden Artists Ltd.

118-119 © John Elk III, Bruce Coleman Inc.*; © Superstock*; WORLD BOOK illustration by Kate Lloyd-Jones, Linden Artists Ltd.

120-125 © Supertock*

126-127 © Superstock*; © George Rockwin, Bruce Coleman Inc.*

128-129 © J.P. Zwaenepoel, Bruce Coleman Collection*; AP/Wide World*; © Joy Spurr, Bruce Coleman Inc.*

132-133 © Superstock*; © Eitan Simanor, Bruce Coleman Inc.*

134-135 © Gerald Cubitt, Bruce Coleman Collection*

136-137 Betsy Day*; © Sharon Smith, Bruce Coleman Inc.*

140-141 © Superstock*; Impressions of the San Francisco Zoo (1989) ink and colors on paper by Wang Yani, Asian Art Museum of San Francisco*

142-143 © Kim Taylor, Bruce Coleman Inc.*; © John Moss, Photo Researchers*

144-145 © Superstock*

148-149 © Superstock*; © Ch. Petit/Vandystadt from Photo Researchers*

152-153 © George Gerster, Photo Researchers*; Atlantide/Amant from Bruce Coleman Inc.*

154-155 © Rick Browne, Photo Researchers*; © Jody Porter, Photo Researchers*; © Superstock*

156-157 © Tim Davis, Photo Researchers*; © Blair Seitz, Photo Researchers*

158-159 © George Holton, Photo Researchers*; © Kevin Rushby, Bruce Coleman Collection*

160-161 © Sharon Smith, Bruce Coleman Inc.*; © Georg Gerster, Photo Researchers*; © Superstock*

164-165 © John Eastcott/VVA Momatiuk from Photo Researchers*; WORLD BOOK illustration by Trevor Boyer, Linden Artists Ltd.

166-167 © Robin Smith, ZEFA*; Carl Purcell*; Photo Researchers*

168-169 © Robert L. Dunne, Bruce Coleman Inc.*; © Tom McHugh, Photo Researchers*; © Tom McHugh, Photo Researchers*; © Dave Watts, Tom Stack & Associates*; © R. Van Nostrand, Photo Researchers*; © Tom McHugh, Photo Researchers*

172-173 © Richard Mikala, Bruce Coleman Inc.*; WORLD BOOK illustration by Walter Linsenmaier

174-175 © Richard Mikala, Bruce Coleman Inc.*; © John Eastcott, VVA Momatiuk from Photo Researchers*; © Dave Watts, Tom Stack & Associates*

178-179 © Gerald Cubitt, Bruce Coleman Collection*; © George de Keerle, Liaison Agency*

180-183 © Superstock*

186-187 WORLD BOOK illustration by Donald Moss*; © Daryl Balfour, Tony Stone Images*

188-189 © Jay H. Matternes*; © Renee Lynn, Photo Researchers*

190-191 © Georg Gerster, Photo Researchers*

194-195 © Bob Burch, Bruce Coleman Inc.*; AP/Wide World*

196-197 © Bob Burch, Bruce Coleman Inc.*; © Jack Vartoogian*

198-199 © Superstock*

200-201 © M. Renaudeau/Hoaqui from Photo Researchers*; © Anup Shah, Animals Animals*

204-205 © Superstock*; © J.C. Carton, Bruce Coleman Inc.*;

208-209 © Superstock*

World Book, Inc. provides high-quality educational and reference products for the family and school. For further information, write World Book Encyclopedia, Attention Customer Service, Post Office Box 11207, Des Moines, IA 50340-1207. Or visit our Web site at http://www.worldbook.com